INNER EXPLORATIONS *of a* SEEKER

Dear Nitasha & Abhomdui,

With warm regards.

Oct 31, 2021

INNER
EXPLORATIONS
of a SEEKER

Amar Ochani

Inner Explorations of a Seeker

For more information, contact the author at
amarochani.com.

ISBN
978-1-7750775-1-0 (Hardcover)
978-1-7750775-0-3 (Paperback)
978-1-7750775-2-7 (eBook)

Published in Canada by Inspired Living Publications,
311-1428 Parkway Blvd., Coquitlam, BC,
V3E 3L8, Canada

In loving memory of my mother and father

TABLE OF CONTENTS

AUTHOR'S NOTE

Like most people, I spent a substantial part of life with the feeling that "something is missing." This feeling stayed with me until I realized that meditation and spirituality interested me more than money and recognition did. Money and fame still pull me, but their lure is far lesser now.

I started writing and sharing these essays in 2014 under the title "Thought for the Week" with a small but diverse group of readers from different backgrounds, age groups, and professions. Their feedback over three years has been very encouraging and deeply humbling. It convinced me that what I wrote and shared was helping people in a small way in their daily lives, as such, it would be good to share this work with a wider audience.

Also, interspersed throughout the book are the daily thoughts I have been writing and sharing over the past year and a half. Every thought dwells on a distinct theme or looks at the same theme from a different perspective, and is complete by itself. They have been arranged, as much as possible, in chronological order. The index of thoughts will be handy to access a specific theme.

When we see life as an open book and the Universe as our teacher, then there are no set rules for learning. We can learn from whoever we come in contact with at any point in time. However, we still need a good teacher to learn the proper technique of meditation. I am fortunate to have learned Vipassana meditation from renowned Vipassana teacher, the late S. N. Goenka. The teachings of the Buddha, which include the practice of Vipassana meditation, have inspired me and continue to illuminate my path. Their imprints will be visible through the pages of the book.

These essays and thoughts are not written for readers of any particular faith, religion, denomination or creed. The themes such as gratitude, love, compassion, self-awareness, mindfulness, meditation, peace, the purpose of life are universal. They can appeal to readers of all faiths and beliefs.

PEACE

When we make peace with ourselves, our
quarrels with the world come to an end.

JOURNEY

If we constantly remember that life is a
journey, we will be very happy travellers.

RECIPE

Selfless actions, healing words, and uplifting
thoughts, these are the ingredients of
the recipe called a beautiful life!

IT'S A NEW DAY

Every new day is a bonus; wages were earned
last night when we went to sleep.

EXTRAORDINARY

If we fill ourselves with ordinary, we will
become ordinary; extraordinary emerges from
the womb of pain and perseverance.

FANTASIES

It's not a problem to build castles in the air; it
becomes a problem when we start living in them.

LETTING GO OF CONTROL

It may sound paradoxical, but when we allow people to be the way they are, it creates an experience of ease and freedom in our own life.

Detachment is more an internal state than an external action. The process of detachment will naturally follow if we untie the inner knot, or at least loosen it a bit. What keeps the knot in place is our compulsive need to control others, particularly our loved ones, and all that under the mistaken belief that we are doing it for their good.

We don't need to go into right or wrong of the control as that will entangle us in arguments, opinions, and conflicting points of view. It would be far more rewarding to see that control doesn't work in the long run, but we come to that conclusion through different routes:

First scenario: We have tried and tried, but it has not worked. However, we do not doubt that control is good for others and sooner or later, they will realize it. We are waiting for them to make mistakes to remind them that had they listened to us, they would have been better off. Obviously, we have not given up control here. We are just biding our time.

Second scenario: We have tried and tried, but it has not worked. However, we are beginning to see the futility of this control business, although we wouldn't mind trying it if it worked. But why lose peace of mind over something that is not yielding any result, hence we stop offering our unsolicited bits of advice. This is a pragmatic approach. The pragmatic approach is like a cease-fire. It may last indefinitely, but one has to guard it all the time. There is a lack of freedom.

Third scenario: While we are on self-imposed censorship with regards to control, we begin to see glimmers of change. As we look closely, we see it is making life easier. The people we thought couldn't survive without our control, have not only survived but are happier and more productive. Moreover, we can see a dramatic shift in our experience over a period. We have more time to follow our interests and do things we are passionate about. We are less anxious, more relaxed. As it gets clearer to us that our desire to control is not helping anyone, we don't want to get into that situation again. From here, it doesn't take much to realize that letting go of control is a better choice, not only for those whom we try to control but also for our own self. In letting go of control, there is freedom for us and others.

Letting go of control should not be misconstrued as being indifferent to the well-being of others, particularly those who are in our life. You don't love them less. It's just that now we are less attached but more available should they need us. We have only removed the spoke from the wheel of life, ours as well as others', to flow and run more smoothly.

ACCEPTANCE

Acceptance is a big energy saver. It consumes a
fraction of energy but lights up our whole world.

WORK

Work is never hard or soft; it becomes
hard when we have no heart in it.

GRATITUDE

We can only strive; it is always someone
else who makes our day.

ART OF LIVING

Too little attention and we lose focus; too much
attention and we get attached; finding the
balance is what the art of living is all about.

WOMEN

If you want to imagine the world without women,
imagine a world without love and light.

WARMTH

Warmth is making people feel at home;
whether it is our house or heart.

SLOW DOWN, PLEASE

It would be unrealistic to deny the pressure of modern life and its associated stress. When we need to run to catch the bus or train in the morning to reach office on time, we must run. But if running to catch the bus or train becomes a daily routine, then we should know something is not right and out of balance. When taking our meals in a hurry becomes a norm, then we should know that we have, perhaps, messed up our priorities. When haste and hustle show up in our every action, we should know we are running in circles.

What do we need to do in our day to day life to experience living in the moment a reality?

Broadly, we live our lives in two modes: One, when we are interacting with the world - work, travel, shopping, socializing, etc., and the other, when we are with ourselves, and there is no compulsion to be time-bound.

To begin with, when we are in the first mode, let the demands of a situation dictate our responses.

Practice, or let's say our self-training to live in the present, begins when we are in the second mode when we are with ourselves, which mostly is when we are at home. Just as we learn to drive a car in slow mode, learning to live in the present too is practised in slow mode.

As we begin to do every activity, perform every action mindfully, and with deliberation, they start to slow down naturally. When we walk, we take every step mindfully, consciously, our walking slows down naturally, and our experience of walking becomes deeper. When we eat, we sit down mindfully to eat, take each morsel of food mindfully, put it in our mouth mindfully, chew it mindfully, and our experience of eating becomes deeper and richer. When we wash our dishes, we wash them mindfully, feeling the water on our hands, the same goes when we are taking a shower or brushing our teeth, combing our hair, applying makeup and so on.

Like any other skill as we become adept and comfortable and start to experience the benefits of slowing down and doing our daily activities mindfully, our faith in the practice will strengthen.

As, when we watch movie scenes in slow motion, they become longer, and our experience of watching richer, slowing down can make every moment longer and our experience of living deeper.

BLESSINGS OF THE PRESENT MOMENT

The past is a memory; the future is an idea; we can live only in the present, in this moment. In a way, we have no choice except to live in this moment. Then why do we find living in the moment so difficult?

One of the reasons we find living in the moment difficult is because we always have this nagging feeling, "Am I missing something?" Or, we are mentally waiting for better things to come up. It is an irony that we spend much of our life "missing out" or "waiting for" while "this moment" is always available to live.

When we are present to and eat our food mindfully with the feelings of gratitude towards nature or God, and the people who made it possible, we will feel relaxed and peaceful. Eating our meals can become a meditative experience. Besides, food will be better digested, paving the way for better health.

INSPIRATION

It is an inspiration, not an explanation
that creates a possibility of change.

BE HAPPY

90% of our worries are about things that may
never happen; the remaining 10% are about
things that have already happened.

PURPOSE OF LIFE

It is when we have discovered the purpose of our life that
we know what we have to keep and what we have to let go.

LOVING KINDNESS

We tend to associate loving kindness with religion, charity, meditation, spirituality, and that is not incorrect. However, loving kindness is much more. Consider the following examples:

> This morning when I reached the elevator of my building, I was surprisingly pleased to see a man waiting with the door open. I expressed my sincere thanks. He said, "I heard the door closing and thought someone must be coming." This is a loving kindness. He was not supposed to wait for anyone, but he still did.

> As I was about to cross the road, a car coming from the side road stopped, and the driver gestured for me to pass. I acknowledged her. She very graciously returned my gratitude with a beaming smile. Neither she nor I was required to acknowledge with kind gestures, but we did. This is a loving kindness.

Two friends were arguing over matter. One of them was so vehement about his point of view that he was ready to bet any amount. The other friend refused to bet but agreed to check it out. Upon checking, he was proved to be correct. When asked, why he didn't bet, he replied, "I knew you were wrong. I did not want to take advantage of your ignorance." This is a loving kindness.

If we cultivate the habit of making room for the mistakes of others, as well as our own, loving kindness will follow. No one is right all the time. Lapses don't have to be equal to punishment; they can be equal to forgiveness. It is not only morally appealing but practically rewarding. If we look around, we may notice that the people we respect the most are not those who believe and practise "tit for tat" or "eye for an eye," but those who forgive others' faults. It is not about doing it right; it is about doing it right with love.

RELAXATION

Relaxation is a choice; stress is a compulsion.

SELF-COMPASSION

Acceptance of one's limitations without the feelings
of guilt or blame is the door to self-compassion.

ENCOURAGEMENT

Encouragement is allowing someone
to discover one's own courage.

JOY

If we make enjoying every moment of life as our main purpose, there will be no room for worries and anxieties to come and build their nest in us.

THE UNIVERSE

Trust the universe; it knows its job well; when nothing seems to be happening on the stage, a lot may be happening behind the stage.

SENSITIVITY

We become insensitive by and by as we walk over things, we can do something about.

JOY AND SORROW

We all seek happiness and joy in our life, but not everyone experiences joy and happiness in their daily living. One may wonder why. Both sorrow and joy reside in the same place - that is in mind. But the frequencies at which we can access them are different.

Sorrow is the by-product of negativities like hatred, greed, ignorance, resentments, ill-will, jealousy, frustrations. They, by their very nature, are gross. It is easier for the mind to get attached to negativities because ordinarily, our minds are gross; the result is the experience of sorrow.

Joy is the by-product of positivities such as love, compassion, generosity, equanimity, optimism, and patience. They, by their very nature, are subtle. Unless we make our minds subtle, it's not possible for us to cultivate these qualities and generate the experience of joy.

Negativities grow on their own. We don't have to make a special effort except to continue to sleep through our ignorance. To develop positive qualities to experience joy in our life, we need to work, not the type of work we do in our mundane life for which our gross minds are adequate, but work that requires introspection, turning inward, to awaken.

First of all, we have to see that there is sorrow and it's not going to go away by fixing external conditions, "If I can get just this thing right!" or "If I owned that car or lived in that house!" or, and this is a big one, "If only my relationship with so and so worked better." They can give us a temporary break, short-lived happiness. However, before long we find ourselves exactly where we were.

Only by facing, realizing and working on the fundamental truth of life that sorrow and its ending, both are within us, we can come to the grip of the real issue.

COMPASSION

If someone is positive, learn from them; if someone
is negative, have compassion for them.

SPIRITUAL

Focus on spiritual, and it will get better and
better as we age; focus on physical, and it
will be pain and more pain as we age.

TASTE

When we eat for the taste, there is no end; when
we eat to live, every food tastes great.

WALKING THE TALK

If we keep closing the gap between our walk and talk,
there will be enough on our plate for quite a while.

EGO

Every interaction that helps me to
dismantle my ego is a blessing.

FORGIVENESS

Forgiveness is not a denial of hurt;
forgiveness is letting go of the hurt.

RELATIONSHIPS

The quality of our relationships is an outcome of our conversation. In common parlance, we understand conversation as the interaction we have with people. Here, the emphasis is more on the internal conversation, our internal dialogue.

Let's do a simple experiment:

Try to picture a person or persons whom you don't quite like. Now listen to your internal dialogue. It is unlikely to be very laudatory of those people.

Now try to picture a person or persons whom you like. You will be beaming with a smile at the very mention of their names.

It's no coincidence that the kind of relationship we have is in sync with our internal dialogue. If our internal dialogue is positive about a person, we will have a warm relationship with that person and vice versa.

But life doesn't run in a straight line. There are ups and downs in relationships. Sometimes, we may find it difficult to appreciate and like people we were very enthusiastic about in the past. If we look closer and try to recreate the internal conversation we had about these people then and the one we have now, we can see the same pattern. We had a very positive internal dialogue about these people then, in contrast to the negative internal dialogue we have now.

Now what we can, and that's what we usually do, is to pick up some incidents and try to rationalize the change in our attitude. By doing so, we will no doubt find ample justification for our actions, but it will create a no-go situation and worsen the relationship as time goes by.

The truth is we can only see what happened. Why it happened is our interpretation of what happened. No one knows the real motivation of others. We have a choice to stick to our interpretation and sacrifice the relationship or look whether there is any other possibility, and there always is one.

The first thing is to honestly accept that I have a dislike or grudge towards another person. If we try to put on a positive show on top of our negative feelings, it's not going to work as the positive will remain tied to the negative. Only truth sets us free to own up to our responsibility.

Each one of us is on a journey where the terrain is unfamiliar and landscape constantly changing, yet we have to walk. We all face and try our best to wrestle with this dilemma. Mistakes are inevitable. By the time we have learned lessons from our past mistakes, we are ready to make new ones.

Forgiveness and loving kindness are the lights that can illuminate our path on this journey. These are divine abidings, and it takes time for us ordinary mortals to cultivate them and make them part of our daily life. Until that happens, grudges are best left alone for the time to take the sting out.

RELATIONSHIPS

Don't press "Delete" too lightly in your life; relationships
are easy to erase but very hard to restore.

LIFE

There always remains something unticked. Life
is like that, and probably, will always be that way.
Accepting the way it is, makes it complete.

INWARD JOURNEY

If we are not mining gold in our inward journey, it
doesn't mean that the direction of our journey is wrong.
It simply means we are not digging deep enough.

PEACE OF MIND

Peace of mind is always waiting at the doorstep;
let go of the ego for peace of mind to come in.

GREATNESS

Greatness is not pie in the sky; greatness is in
practising courtesy and kindness in everyday life.

TRIBUTE

The best tribute we can pay to those we love and admire
is to try doing some of what we love and admire in them.

When we learn to be with uncomfortable feelings and emotions, we have come a long way to be with the flow of life. Then we can see how uncomfortable feelings and emotions gradually start to melt away, giving place to feelings of peace, just like darkness gives way to light gradually with the rising sun.

To be with the flow of life is an ability to accept both sides of life, the ability we can develop through practice. It seems difficult and arduous in the beginning, but gradually we begin to get a handle on it. When you lose awareness of the practice, just smile and come back to be with whatever feeling or emotion you are going through at the moment.

Being in tune with life helps us to develop a holistic view of life. The holistic view doesn't exclude worldly responsibilities. It integrates worldly and spiritual sides of life and helps us to live life fully.

LIGHT

How wonderful it would be to turn on the inner light
when we see the darkness within, as we naturally turn
on the outer light when we see the darkness without.

WAY

We don't lose our way all at once; we just stop paying
attention to our internal radar over a period.

CLARITY

External answers give us false clarity;
real clarity lies within us.

THE UNIVERSE

The Universe knows when we are ready
and for what; we are never alone.

INTERDEPENDENCE

Interdependence is a fact of modern life. However,
when we depend on others for things we can
do, it robs us of an opportunity to discover our
potential and know our limitations.

RIGHT TO LIVE

Every living being has the same right to live; this
is true of ants as it is true of human beings.

LOVE AND ITS MANY SHADES

Love is a feeling, not a thought. We don't think love; we feel love. Thoughts are the preserve of the mind, and mind always wants to know the reasons. We feel feelings in our bodies and hearts; feelings don't wait for reasons to manifest.

When we are in love with someone or something, we don't see the faults. Even when we see the faults, they don't make a dent in our love. True love sees only beauty. To be in love is a privilege and a reward in itself.

Devotees will continue to have an abiding faith and love for God irrespective of what they get in return. There is an old song that reflects the sublime nature of love through these words: "I love your flowers, I love your thorns, give me whatever you want to give, O Sustainer of the world."

Love is based on trust, not conditions. We all know the quality of parents', particularly mother's love for her children. It's unconditional in the beginning, unconditional in the middle, and unconditional in the end.

Love accepts the people as they are, irrespective of their colour, caste, religion, gender, nationality or sexual orientation. Those who have a deep love for humanity know full well the prevalence of evil and selfishness, violence, and cruelty in the world, but that does not stop them from being kind and compassionate to one and all.

Love based on external beauty, in fact, is an attraction or infatuation, which, by its very nature is short-lived. We come across so many couples where we can't find a logical explanation for their being together; there we forget that outer appearance is transitory; the heart sees the inner beauty that the mind cannot. It's not that love is blind. On the contrary, one who is truly in love gets the third eye, which can see the quality of the soul residing in the body.

Is it then the case of either you love, or you don't? Yes and No. Yes, because if you don't feel the love inside your heart at present, that is the truth and we must be honest about it. No, because love can, and more often than not, grows over time. With patience, we can develop a love of God, nature, humanity, persons, ideas, activities, and much more.

Compassion, gratitude, generosity, forgiveness, kindness, appreciation, empathy too are different shades of love and can be developed and felt with an intensity which can become a source of joy and bliss for all those who are touched by them.

ACCEPTANCE

Do what you can; accept what you get.

LOVE

Love is to Listen; love is to care; love is to be present.
Love is the space to think, speak, and act from.

BALANCE SHEET

Our mind is wired to think gains and losses in
material terms, no wonder the balance sheet of our
life never tallies. When we begin to see gains and
losses in non-material terms: peace, happiness,
love, and so on, things start to fall into place.

LET GO

You will know how to let go when you let go.

TRUTH

The truth hurts, but only once; untruth
keeps hurting all the time.

HEALTH

Good health is a means to an end; making it one's
sole preoccupation is like getting on the train
and not knowing where one wants to go.

GRATITUDE

Gratitude is the child of faith; faith in the fairness and benevolence of the Universe and its laws. Things happen for a purpose, although it may not be clear at the moment. If we rewind and replay the movie of our life, we will get the idea of why things happened the way they happened and in most part, we will be grateful that they happened the way they did.

The attitude of gratitude is not inborn; it is cultivated. The mind will try to show us how things are not working, how people are unfair and mean, how life has denied us our rightful place. Thinking and talking in this vein can give us a lot of agreement around, but it may not give us peace which gratitude alone can provide.

How to cultivate gratitude?

When you catch yourself daydreaming and fantasizing, observe the things you are fantasizing about the most. Chances are you want to have more of what you already have, more money, bigger or more houses, better or more cars, holidays in exotic places, more fame and praise, more power and prestige, and so on. Now, let's come back to the present. We may find, to our surprise, that what we indeed want from the "more...," i.e. peace and comfort, happiness and joy, sharing and caring, having a sense of meaning in life, we can very well get from what we already have!

Gratitude comes from an appreciation of what we have. It teaches us humility as we realize the contribution of others in our life and gives us the strength to accept our limitations. It brings forth compassion for the less fortunate. The practice of gratitude can free us from craving for more, which is the source of all suffering.

CONTENTMENT

Life is wonderful when all I need is what I have.

GENUINE

People are genuine when they feel safe with us.

WORRY

Worry is creating an issue where none exists.

SHARE

When you share or give something to someone
they are not ready for; you are doing it for yourself;
when you share or give something to someone
they are ready for, you are doing it for them.

RESPECT

When you respect someone for what they are, it
will always work out; when you respect someone
for what they have, it will never work out.

SUFFERING

Suffering continues until the complete truth is
told; not so much to others, but to oneself.

FORGIVENESS

"Forgiveness liberates the soul." – Nelson Mandela

Human beings are designed to forgive if they will let their fundamental nature prevail. To forget is part of human nature, and what we forget can be easily forgiven if only we don't try to keep our hurt and resentment alive by putting energy into them. For example:

"He has treated me so unfairly; I will never forgive him" or "She has sullied my reputation; I am going to settle the score with her one day!" But like everything else, feelings also change. As time passes by, I may not be thinking so strongly about him or her, but forgiveness doesn't stand a chance if I keep reminding myself time and again of promises to settle scores.

It happens not only on an individual level but also on the collective level. Revenge and vendetta among nations, societies, and religions are kept alive and passed on from generation to generation although the reasons might have all but disappeared.

It's not reasons but our ego that keeps our will, our desire to seek the revenge in place. But ego comes with a cost. A big ego comes at a bigger cost! When we see the cost and futility of wasting energy on the issues that no longer have relevance, the process of forgiveness begins. Then time gets a chance to complete the work of healing as we are no longer pouring energy into resentments and grievances.

GENEROSITY

We are generous when we are at peace.

THE UNIVERSE

When we earnestly invoke the Universe to
show us the way when we can't, it will.

JUDGEMENT

When we see people as human beings, there
are no judgments; when we see people as their
identities, there are only judgments.

FORCE

We force things when we forget there exists
a better option in acceptance that can
accomplish the very things we want to achieve
through force, but in a much better way.

CARE

Things we care about are the things we remember
most; care more to remember more.

DISCRIMINATION

Without developing discrimination between right and
wrong, it's not possible to lead a peaceful life; ends justify
the means attitude results in pain, sooner or later.

ATTACHMENT

We all agree that attachments lead to suffering, and yet, we find it difficult to let go of our attachments. Change from attachment to non-attachment is a gradual process, not the flash of lightning.

If we take a closer look, we can easily see that by being attached, we neither help ourselves nor others. When we are attached to a task or the outcome of our efforts, we are less effective as attachment robs the mind and body of their efficient functioning.

When we are attached, we are less happy, more anxious.

All attachments are an extension of our basic attachment to "I," and "I" is a fiction. Like all fictions, it's unreal but pleasurable. Since it's pleasurable and very deeply entrenched in our psyche, it's not going to go away in a hurry. It will take us a lot of work. However, this work can be done only in human birth, and we are fortunate to have that opportunity.

Non-attachment is freedom. It is an expansion of who we are. Non-attachment doesn't mean cold indifference. It means love and compassion that is not attached to its object.

I, ME, & MINE

In every internal dialogue, every fantasy we have or imaginary script we write, all characters keep changing like musical chairs, except one character, the hero, and that's always "Me!"

If I do something wrong, I have justification. If others do wrong, they are morons. If I do something right, it's due to my exceptional judgment. If others do something right, they must have some motive behind it. We always tend to take a high moral ground and put ourselves on a pedestal.

If my near and dears come to grief, it's serious. If someone else goes through similar misfortune, it's passing news.

Similarly, my views, my religion, my philosophy is always right. Our attachment to these concepts is even clingier. How do we loosen the grip of "I" "me" and "mine," getting rid of them is a far cry?

The first thing is to be aware of the stranglehold that "I" has over us. You will find that in every scene "I" somehow creeps in and it does this so stealthily that we hardly notice. We notice it only when it has entrenched itself deeply in a situation. Before that happens, we need to see the mind's game and realize that it's not funny. It obscures our judgment and creates a camouflage which doesn't allow us to see the reality. It hides the cobwebs in our closet.

What is the reality? When we take a hard look at what is going on inside us, it dawns on us that all that glitters is not gold. It is not very comfortable to look at our weaknesses. There is a tendency to shy away from this confrontation and use various methods to keep up the facade, such as blaming the circumstances, hardships we have gone through to reach where we are today, and so forth. It may help us in gaining temporary truce, but they come back to harass and challenge us again and again. We need to stand our ground and look at our weaknesses and defilements directly in their eyes when they arise. It weakens their force.

When we are conscious of our unwholesome thoughts and tendencies, and we are not sweeping them under the carpet, we will be hesitant to put "I" on a high pedestal. Also, we won't be quite willing to support "I" when it tries to point the finger at others. With practice, we can succeed in deflating the "I" balloon.

EGO

What we think is difficult may well turn out to be easy if we unseat our ego from the driver's seat.

RENUNCIATION

As long as we find mundane life enticing, the joy of renunciation will continue to elude us.

HURT

When we pay attention to how we feel when others hurt us; we will start paying attention to how others feel when we hurt them.

MORE

We can always do more, but what may be
sometimes useful to ask is, "for what?"

MISTAKES

Every mistake should change us a bit, teach
us a bit, and make us a little bit more humble.
If it doesn't, then we are not awake.

POSSIBILITY

Paying less attention to what "should be" and more
to what "could be" can save us a lot of grief.

HOW TO RESPOND
INSTEAD OF REACTING

We will examine this on three levels: action, word, and thought.

The reaction is unconscious. The one who is reacting has little control at the moment of reaction. The first thing is to be conscious of how unconsciously we react.

As we begin to see how automatically we react, we will notice that our reactions have slowed down creating a possibility of pause before reacting. The pause allows us to react consciously; we can also say that pause allows a reaction to turn into a response. It is not possible to observe our reactions when we are in a hurry. One doesn't have to rush things all the time. It's more of a compulsion than necessity. We take this compulsive behaviour everywhere we go, even on our holidays!

Consciously slowing down is not the same as dullness. It's awareness. When we do things with awareness, we can observe things, including our reactions, much better, creating a possibility of that valuable pause we discussed above.

Speaking is the function of listening. More attentively we listen, more effectively we can respond and communicate. Our listening is often marred by the constant chattering of our mind. We are then no longer available. Being present is pre-requisite to good listening and responding thoughtfully.

Now, we come to the thought level. Generally speaking, we give attention in the order of actions, words, and thoughts; which is opposite of how it should be: Thoughts, words, and actions. Thoughts are the source of our words and actions.

We cannot see our reflection in the muddy waters. We need to allow mud to settle down. Similarly, when thoughts are racing and creating ripples in our mind, it's not possible to think straight and take proper action. We need to have patience and allow some time to clear the mind.

Patience comes through practice and from observing how impatient we are and what is the cost of our actions springing from impatience. As we begin to see the cost, change will come, and gradually patience will replace impatience; calmness will replace the mind's agitation.

The actions and the words which will emerge from the calm and serene mind will be thoughtful responses, not automatic reactions.

INTENTIONS

We cannot guarantee that what we say or do will
not be misunderstood, but we can guarantee
that what we say and do is well-intentioned.

GREATER CAUSE

If you cannot see a cause greater than yourself in
whatever you are engaged in, try to make one up.

COMPLAINTS

Most of our complaints will go away if we remember that,
fundamentally, one individual has no right over another.

THOUGHTS

What we say and do matter, but what
we think matters most.

TWO SIDES

Unless we experience suffering, we will not
know what love is, unless we experience fear,
we will not know what courage is.

SMILES

Everything passes away; nothing remains the same.
When we don't turn it into a mantra but live by it,
there are fewer regrets, more smiles in our life.

STOP & GO

It's very important to question from time to time what we are doing, where we are going, choices we are making. Ideally, one should articulate one's purpose of life as best as one can for that will ensure we don't get into activities or endeavours that don't serve the purpose of our life or lead us in the direction of our goals.

However, it's inevitable that we will make mistakes or deviate from our purpose sometimes. Such times are an opportunity to reflect and reconnect with our purpose and goals.

When we are in tune with our purpose, we feel alive and optimistic; we have a feeling of being on the right track. When we have deviated from our purpose, we feel as if we have lost our way, taken a wrong turn. It's natural that one would feel a bit out of water when starting something new, but if the feeling persists, it›s time to sit back and reflect.

What can bring us back on track is no different from what we do when we take a wrong turn on the road: We pull over our vehicle on the side, review our destination and route, turn around our vehicle if necessary and resume our journey.

It is the same for reconnecting with our purpose, except that here we have to deal with our ego, which makes it difficult to accept our mistakes. What can help us to get the better of our ego is to look at the big picture and do some hard and honest thinking about what is important for us. Soon it will become clear that it's best to turn around and follow the route that will reconnect us with the purpose of our life. It's time for renewal.

SMART

Smart is to discover what makes us happy, and then do it.

ILLUSION

Change of scene is not a bad idea; it may even be necessary sometimes, but to hope that the change of scene will give us lasting peace is an illusion.

MISTAKES

More thought we put, fewer mistakes we will make.

EARTH DAY

As a mother as nature, love without boundaries.

FORGETFULNESS

Give up fear of forgetting, and you will remember.

ANGER

The first victim of our anger is the
ability to think of our own good.

SELF-AWARENESS

When we are self-aware, we have gone beyond the push and pull of our mind because we have then successfully created a distance between us and our thoughts, feelings, and emotions. It's like finding the centre to observe our world from, watching a movie from the vantage point without getting involved in the scenes.

This kind of experience may be momentary, intermittent or may last for a longer period. Even when this experience lasts for a very short time, its impact is powerful, the same as when we taste sugar for the first time - we can never forget its sweetness.

It's hard to generate such experiences when our thoughts are racing. We need to slow down to learn to watch the state of our mind. Slowing down our activities allows us to develop self-awareness. Things, thoughts, and feelings will happen exactly the way they were happening earlier, but now they are happening in the light of self-awareness, a world of difference!

How does being self-aware help us in our day to day life?

Our interactions with people will become more thoughtful, less reactive. If I am harbouring any ill will or grudge against someone I am interacting with, I would know when such feelings are arising, and I would be careful in choosing my words and actions. I would be more respectful and humble. This attitude will not go unnoticed. It will generate spontaneous reciprocity and cordiality.

Good health is a function of listening to our body. As we develop the faculty of self-awareness, we will be able to pay attention to what our body is saying more distinctly. We will stop over-eating when our body is saying "enough." We will not stress our body when it's crying for rest; we will inhale more fresh air and drink more water when it is pleading for more oxygen and getting dehydrated.

When we are self-aware, we are less likely to be carried away by our self-critic whose job is to nag us constantly for not being good enough. With self-awareness come self-esteem, peace, and compassion.

BIG PICTURE

Looking at the big picture when we are stuck
blows away the issues we are stuck with
as the wind blows away dry leaves.

OBSTACLES

Every obstacle in our life comes with the
promise of taking us higher and higher.

CRAVING

Craving mostly plays out in the realm of thoughts.
"Wish I had this," "wish I had that." It's strange
that we keep sowing the seeds of suffering for
something we are unlikely to reap benefits of.

DIVERSITY

No two persons are alike, nor are they entirely different;
first makes life interesting, second makes us humble.

KARMA

It's not what we say or do, but the intent
which determines our karma.

FREEDOM

Freedom comes from realizing that there is a lot
we can do nothing about; what then remains
is more than we can do something about.

GENEROSITY

In his famous quote, Andrew Carnegie, a Scottish-American industrialist, business magnate, and philanthropist said, "The man who dies thus rich dies disgraced." These words continue to inspire philanthropists across the world. Its purport seems to be that one who died rich did not use his wealth to do good and earn merits in this world and beyond. What a colossal waste of an opportunity!

On the other hand, there are wealthy people who have given away or pledged all or much of their wealth to charities. Their wisdom and vision are praise-worthy and inspiring.

At the same time, not everyone is wealthy, and one doesn't have to be wealthy to give. Giving is an attitude that one cares. It's a stand that an individual can make a difference. How that stand will show up in the world will differ from person to person.

One will share her or his material wealth. Another will share one's talent, time or other resources. For, one can give what one has, and everyone has something to give, except that many of us don't think it's our job, and that someone else will do it. "I have enough on my plate" or "I have my family to look after." It will be an interesting revelation if we take a few moments to look at how much thought we put into spending for an evening out and how much we think before giving a much lesser amount for some cause.

"But really, my situation is different. I have nothing to share, no money, no time, no nothing." This too is not true. We all have a very precious resource: Vibrations of loving kindness, compassion, and love. And when they flow from the pure heart, they are no less valuable than any other wealth.

LIFE

Life is like a flowing river. It is when we try to hold on to our experiences that it gets muddy.

PURPOSE

Everything, animate or inanimate, has a purpose. It can save us a lot of trouble if we know the purpose before we act.

FAITH

Faith in the fairness of the Universe and its laws comes before it starts revealing its plan to us.

UNIVERSAL GOOD

We tend to think "Everything happens for good"
as personal good; the one who coined the phrase
was probably thinking of universal good.

MAKE YOUR DAY

If we pay close attention to what makes or mars our day,
we will be surprised how achievable it is to make our day.

DHARMA

First, we work to develop dharma in us; then
dharma works to show us the way.

MAGIC OF ACKNOWLEDGMENT

Human beings are born with an urge to make a difference. And, when their contribution is acknowledged, they feel satisfied and validated. If we take a moment and recall the time or occasion when we truly experienced a sense of fulfillment and gratitude, we may find it was a time when people sincerely and honestly acknowledged us for having made a difference in their life. What is true for us is true for others as well. Then, why don't we acknowledge people as much as we should?

- Fear, if we acknowledge people, they will get the upper hand, or they may take advantage of us.
- Why should I acknowledge people? No one acknowledges me.
- The tendency to take people and things for granted.
- Having resentments or grudges.
- Unwillingness to go beyond one's comfort zone.

- Resignation, "What difference does it make whether I acknowledge or not?"

Whatever may be our reasons or justifications for not acknowledging, the cost as regards to satisfaction and aliveness is not worth paying for. When we acknowledge people, they feel inspired to do better and reciprocate with humility. Our relationships can be far more satisfying and be nurturing; the atmosphere in homes more harmonious and peaceful; workplaces more productive and motivating.

We do acknowledge and appreciate people in our life but perhaps not sufficiently and consciously. Gratitude is the seed of acknowledgment. Listening and being present is essential. Little things like saying "thank you" and "sorry" with sincerity and feeling can come across as an acknowledgment. Genuinely appreciating someone for what one has said or done, small or big, is an acknowledgment and could be a reason for the smile on someone's face. Recognizing an employee, a colleague or a friend and acknowledging their contribution can be highly motivating and inspiring. Sincerity and willingness to recognize others' contribution in our life is the key. And, we don't have to wait until someone has done something or said something, just having someone in our life could be the most important contribution and worthy of acknowledgment.

Where to begin? Family, we tend to overlook the contribution of those who are closest to us. It's the family where we find it difficult to practise acknowledgment. This may sound strange, but it's true as over time we get set in our ways, it becomes quite challenging to make changes in the way we treat and interact with each other in the family. However, if we sit back and do a little introspection, it would become clear to us that it's worth going through a bit of awkwardness and relating newly to our family.

As we see our relationships changing for better with the practice of acknowledgment, it will become a natural expression of the way we relate to people irrespective of whether they are our near and dear ones or strangers. Acknowledgment creates the bond of respect and love between giver and receiver. One doesn't have to analyze people to acknowledge them. Just removing filters of judgment, accepting people as they are is sufficient to create an opening.

Also, never forget to acknowledge yourself for having made a difference. It is not conceit. It is self-awareness. It helps to enhance our self-esteem and gives us confidence in our ability to bring about positive changes in our life, and the lives of others.

POTENTIAL

When we underestimate people,
they tend to prove us right.

SOLITUDE

In solitude, you meet the one you have
been missing all along: Yourself.

COMPASSION

Compassion should follow acceptance;
this is the test of true acceptance.

LOVE

If we wait for the ill will and animosities to go
away completely before we express our love in the
world, we will be waiting for a long, long time.

WRONGDOING

Wrongdoing catches up at some point in our life,
no matter how hard we try, how clever we are.
This is the law of nature beyond negotiation.

NEEDS

If we don't hold onto things, the unnecessary
ones will drop out; what will remain is
what we need, and that is not much.

TRILOGY

Expectations are rooted in need; faith frees us, and contribution fulfills us.

TRILOGY-I
EXPECTATIONS

Expectations are the main source of suffering. The fewer expectations we have, the happier we will be. But our everyday living is so inextricably tied to expectations that it would be unrealistic to think that we can live without expectations just by wishing so.

Expectations are of two kinds. The common expectations: We expect to return home in the evening when we leave for work in the morning, see our car at the spot we parked it in, get our pay cheque at the end of the week or month, and so forth.

These are just a few examples of common expectations. There are much more to our everyday living. As a matter of fact, we don't even consider them as expectations. We take them for granted. We realize their true nature only when something goes wrong, and our routine gets disrupted. In the given examples, we may realize our underlying expectations if our car is stolen, our home is damaged or if we lose our job.

However, when not fulfilled, the impact of the common, day-to-day expectations is at a surface level. They cause a temporary setback, disturbance or turmoil for sure but get fixed sooner or later. They don't make inroads at a deeper level of our consciousness.

Others are psychological expectations. The psychological expectations arise, consciously or unconsciously, when we perform what we believe are our disinterested or unselfish actions, but their true nature is revealed when underlying expectations are not met. It could happen, for instance, when we are interacting with our families, with our friends, within our workplaces, voluntary organizations, with neighbours, or getting into new relationships. We should look closely at our motivation when performing actions that we believe are selfless and altruistic because if we don't, our hidden expectations for the name, fame, approval, acknowledgment or material gain will become fertile ground for suffering.

We should closely scrutinize every assumption of the selfless act. It will help us in two ways: Firstly, if we see the seeds of self-interest in our action, we could either abstain from performing it or postpone its performance. It would give us time to reflect upon and purify our motivation of selfish intent. Once we have purified our motivation of selfish expectations, there is no possibility of suffering. Such action will only bring joy and happiness to us and others.

Secondly, if we cannot abstain or postpone acting but become aware of our self-serving bias after reflecting upon it, that too is not bad, because we can work with something that we are aware of as opposed to something of which we are not aware. As we go along, our expectations will become weaker and weaker in the light of awareness and our experience of whatever we are engaged in will become more fulfilling.

TRILOGY-II
FAITH

In the first part of the trilogy, we saw how expectations lead to suffering. At this stage, it would be fair to ask that if we let go of our expectations, where do we get our motivation from, or how do we put power behind our actions? It's true that we need to power our actions with energy. Otherwise, our actions become listless and ineffective. We can accomplish this by replacing expectations with faith. Faith can be our powerful friend.

Nothing much can be achieved for our good, or the good of others, without having faith. Actions based on expectations lead to suffering; actions grounded in faith lead to freedom from suffering.

For the vast majority of us, however, our faith is what our religion says. Religious or sectarian faith, with its rituals and ceremonies, traditions and beliefs, breeds more expectations. While there is nothing wrong in rituals and ceremonies, there is a possibility of us losing our way if we begin to equate these with spirituality.

We need faith based on universal principles, the law of nature which is straightforward and simple, "As you sow, so shall you reap." It applies to all, irrespective of race, religion, colour, nationality, gender, or position. When we get anchored in the law of nature, we can perform our actions with confidence, not with anxiety, because we would know beyond the shadow of a doubt that there cannot be any foul play here. Life can get easier when we know our case is in the hands of an impartial judge who can neither be appeased nor intimidated.

Faith in the infallibility and immutability of the law of nature can provide a solid foundation for our actions. It doesn't matter what name we give to that power as long as we don't make it into a sectarian thing and our faith is unshakable.

The Universe is a wonderful companion; it's always on our side when we are on the right path, and cautions us when we are not. Once we have developed faith in the benevolence of the Universe and try making it a part of our everyday living, we don't have to look to others for approval or vindication of our position. Our experience of life would tell us whether we were operating from expectations or faith.

TRILOGY-III
CONTRIBUTION

As our faith in the fairness of the Universe gets strengthened, our actions are less and less propelled by expectations. When we shift from expectations to faith, the stage is set for contribution. The contribution is the fulfillment of our potential as human beings.

The contribution is a choice. One can live life in comfort, attending to one's concerns and interests without developing or articulating one's vision of contribution, and that wouldn't be wrong either. It is just that making a difference satisfies the basic urge of human beings. It brings out the real human being hidden within one's identity.

Siddhartha Gautama, who became the Buddha, could have lived his entire life in the luxuries and comfort of his palaces, but he chose to leave everything behind and go in search of ultimate truth. When he became the Buddha, he could have spent his entire life in supreme bliss, but he chose to remain in the world to teach dharma to the suffering humanity.

Mahatma Gandhi could have lived comfortably and pursued his successful practice as a barrister, but he chose to throw himself, heart and soul, in India's struggle for freedom.

Nelson Mandela and Martin Luther King Jr. could have lived their life well toeing the line of powers that be, but they decided to swim against the current and lived and died in the pursuit of their dreams.

Of course, not everyone is the Buddha, Mahatma Gandhi, Nelson Mandela or Martin Luther King Jr., and we need not be the one to make a difference.

When we are economizing on the use of water, electricity, gas, paper, etc., we are helping conserve limited natural resources besides helping reduce global warming. When we avoid wasting food, we are contributing towards the end of hunger on the planet. When we don't discard the appeals received from the charities right away but reflect upon them to see how best we can help within our means, we are making a difference in the lives of less fortunate or contributing towards the advancement of some cause.

We are contributing towards creating a cordial atmosphere around us when we refrain from engaging in gossiping and backbiting and show courtesy and consideration to others. The words can heal, and words can hurt. When we use words with care and commitment, they can not only heal but also create mutual trust, respect, amity, and good will.

Our attitude is no less important than our words and actions towards building healthy and harmonious relations. When we stop judging and comparing, we are sending positive vibes to those who we come in contact with. A "Who am I to judge?" attitude can end all quarrels and dramatically improve our relationships.

We often wait for an ideal time to take the initiative or to make a beginning. These beautiful quotes sum up as to when is the right time to wake up to our power to make a difference: "A journey of a thousand miles begins with a single step." - Lao Tzu; "Do what you can, with what you have, where you are." - Theodore Roosevelt

NON-VIOLENCE

Every unwholesome thought, word, and
action is violence; we need to be more than
vegetarian to be truly non-violent.

SELF-ACCEPTANCE

There will always be a gap between what we are
and who we want to become as a person. However,
the progress towards who we want to become is
possible only when we accept what we are.

BLESSINGS

The surest thing that can take us out of misery,
whenever it shows its face, is to count our blessings.

TO EACH HIS OWN

"To each his own" when practised with
compassion unites; "To each his own" when
practised with indifference, divides.

JOY

Joy follows sorrow as sure as day follows night; the
former we often forget, the latter we never doubt.

INNER VOICE

When we are attached to our agenda, we
tend to ignore our inner voice.

HOW TO FIND YOUR PASSION

Our career choices and priorities, interests and hobbies, for the most part, are externally determined. The family background, parents' expectations, what society considers as a measure of success, peer pressure, current fads - they all combine to send unmistakable signals and cues to a new aspirant to fall in line to survive. Happiness and fulfillment are assumed to fall out from success, money or fame. Unfortunately, this is not true. History is replete with examples of those who found to their dismay that money, fame, and success are poor indicators of happiness.

How do we discover our passion and live the life we love?

- If we have not found our passion, it's unlikely we are experiencing real happiness and ease in our life. Introspection will help. We need to be honest about our feelings and experience of life.

- Observing what we enjoy doing. What kinds of subjects or themes are important to us that we keep returning to again and again in our life?

- We will find that we come alive when we are engaged in those subjects and activities.

- When we are passionate about a topic, activity or theme, we get naturally drawn to it.

There could be many more clues. Once you have discovered your passion, don't let it go regardless of what stage you are at in your life. Blessed are those who find their passion at an early stage in life, doubly blessed are those who follow through their passion.

Do we have to leave everything and follow our passion? These are the details that each one of us must work out individually. If it entails a change in career path, then obviously, one has to make preparations with due regard to the timing. Having gained the clarity, however, one should resolutely follow through and do what one needs to do.

In many cases, all we need to do is to rearrange our priorities. For example, if I discover that music is my passion, all I need to do is to make music the top priority in my life and everything else secondary to the music. Once I am clear about this, everything else will fall into place. It doesn't mean I will shun my family, job or social responsibilities, although it does mean I will make time for socializing when my music schedule and commitments permit. Also, I may have to do few other changes in my life. But, if I am clear that this is what I want to pursue in life, I wouldn't feel this as a burden. Initially, one may have to go through some adjustment process, however, soon it will become a normal thing, and everyone will accept it if one is clear, sincere, and determined.

One can use the above example for anything that makes one happy and gives one joy of fulfillment. As Mark Twain said, "The two most important days in your life are the day you are born, and the day you find out why." These words are worthy of being enshrined in gold.

Having rearranged our priorities, we will soon discover that we can perform our duties more efficiently while at the same time progress on our new path for the simple reason that we have removed the contradictions and rebalanced our priorities making them consistent with our inner urge and aspirations. We are finally doing what we always wanted to do. We have discovered the love of our life. Our experience of life will become authentic.

TRUST

Trust is often the missing link that
can open the door to success.

POSSIBILITY

The best way to create a new possibility for
the day is to start the day with yourself.

CHARACTER

The character is built by making a habit of doing
the right thing when no one is looking.

THOUGHTS

To see that a weak thought leads to a weak action, and vice versa is the game changer.

HONESTY

Honesty without courage is a lost virtue.

MIND

The mind will always try to keep us under the illusion that we can eat the cake and have it too. Life is about the choices, to get something, we must let go of something else.

WHY BE AWARE?

We see an object say a car; we become conscious of the car. We hear music; we become conscious of music. If we look into our everyday experience, we will notice that we are present to an object momentarily as we become conscious of the object. But soon this presence is lost, and the mind starts overlaying its ideas and interpretations on it. The result is that we drift into the direction of our mind and start seeing things through the lenses of the mind.

We are not talking about this momentary presence which comes as soon as we become conscious of something. The presence we are talking about is the intentional act of keeping our attention on the activity or an experience we are going through without being distracted by the intrusion of irrelevant thoughts.

Before we continue, it would be worthwhile to ask the question: "Why be aware?"

When we are aware of our thoughts and observe them with sustained awareness, they lose their power to distract us from our present experience. Even if we are not able to free ourselves entirely from their stranglehold, being constantly aware of thoughts will alert us to pay more attention to the activity or interaction we are engaged in. It will make a qualitative difference in our experience. Let's take a couple of examples:

We are listening to a speaker who reminds us of our school teacher. Our mind would rush out all the good and bad memories of our school days. If we are not watching our thoughts, we will get lost in them and hardly listen to the speaker. But if we are aware of our thoughts, we will be alert and listen more attentively to the speaker. Now we are in control, not our random thoughts.

You are looking at a painting in a museum. You become conscious of it. It is a painting. No sooner have you started looking at it, a thought comes to your mind - "This looks like a painting I saw in the mall." If you are aware of your thought, you will keep it at bay and prevent it from distracting you from enjoying the painting. But suppose you are not observing your thoughts - "This looks like a painting I saw at the mall... I wanted to buy that painting... but the price was too high... and the salesperson was not very convincing..." Now, the mind has taken over. We are still looking at the painting, but we are looking at the painting from a distorted view like one looks at the moon through the clouds.

To observe one's thoughts is a useful tool to develop the faculty of awareness. We learn it through trial and error. Persistence is the key.

Being mindful of our daily activities is also helpful in enhancing our awareness. If we see our mind has wandered away while eating, we bring it back to eating, but with the awareness that by doing so we are training our mind. While walking if we notice our mind has wandered away, we steer it back to walking, but with the awareness that by doing so we are training our mind. Never lose sight of the purpose, lest the practice becomes mechanical, a mindless watch.

Living life mindfully and with awareness is not a luxury but a necessity, which we all need to experience newness in everyday living.

IRONY

It is an irony that no one has ever turned the clock
back or moved it forward, and yet, we live more
in the past or the future than in the present.

APPROVAL

No one knows us better than we know ourselves; then
why wait for the world to tell us we are good enough.

GAME

At the end of the day, life is a game where playing
is more important than winning or losing.

DO WHAT YOU LOVE

When we do what we love, then love
reminds us of what we have to do.

SOLITUDE

Solitude is the soul of awakening.

PURPOSE

When we know the purpose of what we
are doing, the mind listens to us.

ATTENTION:

KEY TO COMPASSION

Compassion is not just feeling sorry or sad. It's not only about the tears welling up in our eyes. His Holiness, the Dalai Lama, has beautifully captured the essence of compassion in these words: "True compassion is not just an emotional response but a firm commitment founded on reason."

To be compassionate, one has to be attentive. How can I be kind to others if I am not thinking deeply about their condition? How can I be compassionate to the sorrows and suffering of others if I am not reflecting on their plight? How can I be committed if I am not able to stand firm in the face of ups and downs or when circumstances change?

We need to develop a mind which can stay on one point for some length of time to generate true compassion that is born out of clear understanding and firm commitment.

There is much suffering in the world. One often gets overwhelmed by the happenings near and far, and start wondering if there is any point in paying attention. True compassion itself is a contribution, and it shows the way. Action may differ from person to person.

True compassion can arise when we pause and reflect, and these are the attributes of an attentive mind.

ENLIGHTENMENT

An enlightened person is subject to the experience of
misery in the same way as an unenlightened person is,
except that enlightened person is aware of his/her misery
and knows it will pass as will the experience of joy.

FATHER'S DAY

Only a mother can tell us how good father is.

GOODWILL

As long as the source of our actions is ill will,
it's not going to work, no matter how beautifully
crafted the words we use are; it's better to
wait until ill will turns into goodwill.

PLANET EARTH

When we consider the countless species that exist as our partners and rightful inhabitants as we human beings are, saving planet Earth becomes a distinct possibility.

PEACE

We abide in peace when we have nothing to prove.

THOUGHTS

Be a good listener to your thoughts, and
the thoughts will be good to you.

GO EASY ON YOURSELF

Have you ever wondered how we convert our mistakes into feelings of guilt and blame? Suppose I have made a wrong purchase decision, and let's say it is not possible to return the item. I realize my mistake only after the article is safely in the bag and money has gone out from my pocket.

To start with, I am feeling uneasy. "Was it a right decision? I am not sure." Slowly, the trend of my thoughts is shifting. "But why do I end up making such stupid mistakes?" or "I should have thought about it" or "I should have taken so and so's opinion." Now, I am feeling miserable. It is not helping me feel better, so I take on the salesperson who sold me the unwanted thing. "That person should not have pressurized me!" or "These salespersons, all they want is to make a sale..." Now, I am feeling more miserable. I have turned what probably was an error of judgment into a psychological warfare of guilt and blame. I am stuck. We keep playing this guilt and blame game in our life, mostly unconsciously.

The past is irreversible, but the consequences of the past can be amenable to correction if we see mistakes as mistakes and not an issue of feeling guilty or blaming others. When we accept our responsibility for a mistake, we don't waste our time and energy dwelling on negative thoughts and words. Instead, we start looking for a solution and how best to learn from our mistakes.

As long as we are living and are in action, we will keep making mistakes. As John Wooden, an American baseball player and coach said: "If you are not making mistakes, then you are not doing anything. I am positive a doer makes mistakes."

EQUANIMITY

It is not in the nature of things that everyone
gets life in a neat package, but with equanimity,
every life can be a bundle of joy.

SETBACKS

Setbacks are often caused when we try to
run when the walk is good enough.

INTEGRITY

Present not lived with integrity comes
back to haunt us as the past.

INNER SPACE

It is okay for the mind to wander away from time
to time; that is its nature. But come back to take
refuge in your inner space to find peace.

SELF-REFLECTION

When ego strikes, remind yourself of
others' achievements; when you see
others' faults, remember your own.

LISTENING

Words are words. It is the listening that fills the words
with energy and makes them inspiring and moving.

RIGHT VIEW

If mind perceives the world to be a safe place and nature a benevolent friend, that is how the world and nature would turn out to be and vice versa.

A very common example of how having a wrong view changes our whole world: If someone sees a rope mistakes it for a snake, their whole mind will be filled with fear. The rope will produce the same effect in them as a real snake would because of their wrong view. Once they recognize a rope as a rope, their fear will disappear because they have a right view now.

Similarly, if I think material things will give me happiness and joy, I will keep accumulating them out of my ignorance of real source of happiness and joy. We need material things for our livelihood for sure, but there is a difference between need and greed. One is a basic requirement; the other is succumbing to our base instinct.

The source of real happiness and joy in our life is to develop a pure mind and generous heart. We cannot purify our mind and be generous in dealing with our fellow beings when ill will and greed are ruling our mind. When we begin to have the right view of life, we change, our priorities change. Then we like to spend our time in a meaningful way. Then we become conscious of the gift this human birth is and how fragile and uncertain this life is. With the development of the right view, we can penetrate the veil of ignorance that keeps us in bondage and herald the dawn of wisdom.

BLIND MEN AND THE ELEPHANT:

REVISITED

Once upon a time, there lived six blind men in a village. One day the villagers told them, "Hey, there is an elephant in the village today." They had no idea what an elephant was. They decided, "Even though we will not be able to see it, let's go and feel it anyway." All of them went and touched the elephant.

"Hey, the elephant is a pillar," said the first man who touched its leg. "No! It is like a rope," said the second man who touched the tail. "Oh, no! It is like a thick branch of a tree," said the third man who touched the trunk of the elephant. "It is like a big hand fan," said the fourth man who touched the ear of the elephant. "It is like a huge wall," said the fifth man who touched the belly of the elephant. "It is like a solid pipe," said the sixth man who touched the tusk of the elephant.

They began to argue, and everyone insisted he was right. A wise man was passing by, he stopped and asked them, "What is the matter?" They said, "We cannot agree on what the elephant is like." Each one of them told what he thought the elephant was. The wise man calmly explained to them, "All of you are right. The reason you are differently telling it is that each one of you has touched a different part of the elephant. The elephant has all those features that you all mention."

"Oh!" everyone said. There was no more fight.

This story and its many versions have been around for millennia, originating in India and then travelling around the world but we, the blind people of the world, continue to believe that our reality - our beliefs, our religion, our culture, our viewpoint - is the only reality. Not only do we believe but are ready to argue, quarrel, fight and even wage wars to prove our point.

Wisdom comes when we realize that we are like those blind men, and our reality will always be partial and limited. With this realization or insight, something begins to shift. The immense diversity in the world with its different races, cultures, religions, and diverse ideologies begins to make sense. An understanding rises, and compassion begins to flow. A deep silence sets in, and one starts to listen and empathize with the dilemma of humanity. Abruptness and impatience give place to appreciation and sympathy. It begins to dawn that salvation is not in attaining perfection but in embracing one's imperfection. And then something magical happens - one begins to see the whole reality.

MIDDLE PATH

Extremes breed conflict and discord; middle
path leads to peace and harmony.

DEAD END

We feel overwhelmed when we think we have reached
the Dead End of a one-way street in our life. However,
we forget that we always have an option to remove that
sign for it is we who have placed it in the first place.

SMILE

We are often discouraged by sad looks; Who knows our
smile will change their world! **So always take chances.**

DREAMS

One goes in the direction of one's dreams not because it is
the right thing to do, but because it's the only thing to do.

UNITY

What can unfailingly unite all human
beings is the truth of suffering.

ADMIRATION

Admiration and love are buddies; we
can't have one without the other.

EQUANIMITY: KEY TO
A BALANCED LIFE

Everyone wants to be happy and lead a peaceful life, but, not everyone has peace and happiness as the dominant experience of their life.

Things that we don't want to happen often happen, making us unhappy; things we do want don't happen, and again, we are unhappy. We have very little if at all, any control over external things.

If we have a pleasant experience, we feel great and crave for more. When it ends, we feel miserable. If we have an unpleasant experience, we want to get rid of it right away but seems like it will never end, and we feel miserable.

Thus, we keep swinging between praise and blame, gain and loss, honour and dishonour, pleasant and unpleasant experiences of life.

Equanimity is the quality of evenness of mind, a state of inner equipoise, which allows us to remain centred in the face of vicissitudes of life. If we get affected and lose balance, it helps us regain our balance.

How to develop and maintain equanimity?

Equanimity is the child of wisdom or insight that all experiences, whether pleasant or unpleasant, are impermanent. They arise, stay for some time, and sooner or later pass away. So why cling to pleasant and have an aversion to the unpleasant? It doesn't make sense.

Telltale signs of impermanence and change are spread all over the Universe: days turn into nights; seasons change, trees shed their leaves and renew themselves, there's a constant flow of humanity, and nothing ever remains the same.

The seed of equanimity once developed into a sapling must be watered with awareness for it to grow and become a benevolent tree that will benefit us as well as others.

CONQUERING THE FEAR OF DEATH

Death is an unknown quantity. The closest we come to death is when one of our loved ones passes on. That is when we come face to face with the reality of death and the impermanence of life. Give us some time, and we are back to normal and life as usual. Life's relentless march towards death goes on unabated. Nothing can stop it, and yet we don't like to face this truth. It is amazing! The more we think about it, more we will find this attitude strange if not bizarre.

Why is it so difficult to come to terms with this reality? Let me ask a question. If I tell someone who wants to learn rock climbing to start at Mount Everest, will he or she not consider the suggestion as preposterous and laughable? And yet, that is what we do to ourselves when it comes to facing the truth of impermanence. To accept death with equanimity, without training our mind to accept the truth of impermanence in our daily life is equally unrealistic.

Nothing lasts. Be it animate or inanimate; everything is subject to the law of impermanence and decay. Every cell of our body is in a state of flux and change. We just have to look at our old pictures to see how much we have changed. Our thoughts, our moods are changing every moment. When we start observing the phenomenon of impermanence in our daily life, we start to build our muscles. Gradually, a realization dawns that change is inherent and decay is embedded in everything. To such degree that we get established in this realization, we get liberated from the fear of death. To use the rock climbing metaphor, conquering Mount Everest wouldn't seem such an intimidating task then.

In his final words, the Buddha said: "Remember, all things that come into being must pass away. Strive earnestly" – *The Dhammapada, Introduced & Translated by Eknath Easwaran*

"Strive earnestly." These are the golden words. We will be much relaxed about death if we continue to deepen our awareness of impermanence in our daily life and strive with earnestness to purify our mind of all defilements. Then there will be no or fewer incompletions lingering in our life. If we were living to our true potential, doing the best we can and accepting with equanimity what we can't, we would be living with peace in this life and look forward to death without regrets as a climax of a life well lived.

THE STORY

The story of our life always remains incomplete
because we don't want to read the last chapter.

EYE-OPENER

When we don't get what we want, we know what we need.

LOVE AND LEARNING

Nature of love and learning is such
that they flow outward.

PEOPLE

Choose the company you keep wisely. You will
have fewer regrets more peace in your life.

INNER SPACE

Our real "home sweet home" is our inner space.

GOOD DEED

Allow yourself to experience happiness when
you do a good deed; you have earned it.

MIRROR

What I see outside is the reflection of what I am inside.

MIRROR-I

When I see envy, jealousy, resentment, and bitterness in people, I am seeing the reflection of what is inside me. On the other hand, if we see loving kindness, generosity, and compassion in people, it's a sign that goodness within us is gaining momentum.

Until we attain nirvana, roots of evil and good, negative and positive will remain within us. However, it's up to us whether we water the roots of evil or good.

We often take pride in our ability to see through people, to judge people, to label people correctly. It is how our mind operates to create the illusion of duality. Although, we cannot deny the physical existence of the outer world, the way we react to the outer world, the way we react to people is the result of our perceptions. It is us who have, consciously or unconsciously, formed our perceptions and it's us who can change our perceptions.

When it dawns on us that negativities we see in others are nothing but our mirror image, we begin to see where the work is required and where we need to focus, but the door is now open for us to step into new possibilities.

We may not like what we see in the mirror and say, "This is a wrong mirror," and go into a deeper illusion; or we can say, "What I see is not pretty, but the mirror can't lie," and begin the work of purification in earnest. The first choice keeps us in ignorance; the latter ushers us into a world of reality where serious work is possible.

It's lifelong work, but it's not the kind of work that gets remunerated at the end of a month or a week, nor do we have to wait until our next birth to reap the rewards. It is the kind of work which gets rewarded here and now. Peace follows purification as sure as a shadow follows substance.

MIRROR-II

"Peace follows purification as sure as a shadow follows substance." This is where we ended the first part of the Mirror. However, if we stop here and wait for some miraculous powers to purify us, we will be waiting in vain because no one can do this work for us. Others who are kind and compassionate and have nothing but love for humanity in their hearts can show us the way, the actual work, however, must be done by us.

Purification is an inside job and peace is the reward for a job well done. If we remove or at least reduce ill will and hatred from our mind and fill it with goodwill and kindness, the result will naturally be the experience of peace and joy. However, we can lay the groundwork for this work only by turning inward. The more time and energy we use in our interactions with the external world, the less we will have to turn inward, to look within.

We must take an honest look at the way we are in the world: our socializing interests, networks we are part of, social media we remain glued. Are they leaving us with sufficient time to spend in solitude? Are they helping us in our "inside job"? Are we left with an experience of peace after these interactions? Are they helping us to make progress on our chosen path or they are pulling us back?

This inquiry should be done continuously for it is inevitable we will make mistakes and get into pursuits that don't serve us. Resetting priorities is an ongoing process. Honesty alone is not sufficient to carry out this process successfully. We need courage along with honesty to put us back on track. We need courage, not so much to overcome external hurdles but to defeat our ego. It's our ego that tries to keep us tied to pursuits that are neither aligned with what matters most to us: to have experience of peace and serenity in everyday living, nor are they required to fulfill our basic obligations in the world.

We don't need to get away from the world, but it is important that we don't get lost in a ceaseless activity that doesn't leave us time to dwell in our inner space, which alone is the ground of peace and serenity.

BLAME

Pointing fingers never work regardless
of whether we are right or wrong.

SOLITUDE

As it takes some time to get to know people and enjoy
their company, it takes time to learn to enjoy our own
company. However, the former comes with a price tag:
likes and dislikes, whereas the latter is priceless!

FANTASY

We fantasize when we want something that
we don't believe is going to happen.

ANGER

Anger itself is a good enough reason to postpone taking
any action irrespective of whether we are right or wrong.

FORGIVENESS

Forgiveness is to let go of hard feelings; it
doesn't stop us from doing the right thing.

PROBLEMS

Most, if not all, our problems with people are due
to our not coming out openly with them; the more
we hide, the heavier the problems become.

TRUTH IS LESS, NOT MORE

To see the truth, we must let go of the stories around the truth. Let's take a look:

We talk about people, events, politics, spirituality, right and wrong based on what we hear and read; what we watch on TV or access through social media. The truth is very simple. They are just our opinions; we don't really know. Being aware of this truth is liberating because then we don't have to carry the burden of our opinions.

Day in and day out, we are bombarded with advertisements and information about the food we should eat, medicines and supplements we should take and so on. One survey tells us we should avoid certain foods. Other survey comes out and advises us to do precisely the opposite of that. The truth is no one knows more about our body than we do. It's just that we don't listen to it. Paying attention to our bodies will reveal what works for us and what doesn't. This is not to say that we will ignore our doctor's advice.

Human beings are interdependent. No doubt about it, but when people become our psychological need, we are not people persons or social-minded. The truth is we have not learned the art of enjoying our own company and developed our inner self-reliance.

It's great to travel, watch movies, enjoy socializing, embark on new adventures, and do a whole lot of other activities. But the truth is, the exhilaration felt through such experiences is transitory and short-lived. To find real happiness, one doesn't have to go anywhere except to turn inward and make a habit of visiting one's inner space.

"The truth shall set you free." True, but for the truth to set us free it has to be our truth seen and experienced within us.

TRUTH & LIE

Both, to tell the truth, and to tell a lie, are easy; except,
it is simpler to live with the truth than with a lie.

MISTAKES

The only way we can learn from mistakes is by not
giving up or losing heart when we repeat them.

LEAP

Fear always comes up when we are about to do
something that is outside of our comfort zone;
taking that leap can open up a new possibility;
not taking that leap is a waste of opportunity.

CRYSTAL BALL

No one has a crystal ball to look into the future; every action results in some unforeseen consequences to be accepted and addressed.

PATH

It's not by digging here, digging there, we get water; we get water by digging deep; the same goes for finding the right path.

AGENDA

Keep dropping your agenda and remain in tune with the flow.

INNER VOICE

The inner voice is more like a navigational tool. It warns us of the hazards ahead or gives us all clear signal. Then, it is up to us whether to take heed or ignore. If we are not accustomed to listening to our inner voice, it would be feeble at best. As we practise listening to our inner voice, it gets loud and clear.

Why is it so difficult to hear the inner voice?

It's difficult to hear our inner voice because our mind is constantly chattering away. We need to look inside whereas we are taught to look outside. On top of all that, we are always in a rush. Advertisements, media, deadlines, competition, and social norms, all combine to create constant noise in our mind. We need to quiet our mind to listen to our inner voice. It is a gradual process; easier said than done, but we can always make a beginning.

How do we recognize our inner voice? We would know when we are listening to our inner voice. Still, there are some pointers:

- Inner voice stands alone. It doesn't need any reasons, justifications or props to stand on.

- Inner voice speaks to you and what you need to do. It guides us to go ahead or go away without guilt or blame.

- The mind will always come with what is good for us, that too for a short term; that's why its lure is attractive and makes listening to our inner voice difficult. Inner voice will be good for us and good for others.

- The mind comes with baggage and tries to drag us in the past. Inner voice points to the future.

- The mind shows us our limitations: "This is not the way to do things; you have never done this before, what is the point?" or "You have already made up your mind," "It would be inconvenient, uncomfortable." Inner voice stands by itself - "This is not the right thing to do, it's not the right time, this is not consistent with who you are" - period.

- The mind will fill us with fear; an inner voice will lead us to freedom from fear.

- Once we have disregarded the promptings of our mind and acted trusting our inner voice, the issue that was perplexing us will get dissolved, and a new opening will get created. We will feel confident that we have done the right thing. We will experience freedom and spontaneity.

The first thing to do when we hear the footsteps of our inner voice is to take a pause. The inner voice is essentially the voice of wisdom. It invites one to look at an issue from more than one angle.

Every step or action we take after listening to our inner voice takes us away from the bondage of our reactive mind and closer to living our lives in a manner consistent with who we are, away from who we always have been and closer to who we could be.

Amar Ochani

FUTURE

When we let future take care of our
worries, it does a wonderful job!

PROVING A POINT

Trying to prove a point is an expensive
hobby; it drains our energy.

SATISFACTION

If our measure of satisfaction is a comparison, we
will always be sitting on the shifting sands.

THOUGHTS & FEELINGS

Like everything else in the Universe, thoughts
and feelings arise and pass away; they torment
us only when we get attached to them.

RIGHT

We do right when we allow the right to lead us.

AWARENESS

Ideas and intentions are important, but what is most important is awareness of what we are doing or thinking right now.

SILENCE, DOOR TO INNER PEACE

Silence is the practice ground for finding inner peace:

- In the midst of arguments, someone has to give rest to one's voice to give peace a chance.
- Whether it is meditation or prayer, we shut down all outside noise to go inside us to find peace.
- For peaceful sleep, silence is a prerequisite.

It is obvious, but we often overlook how we can use the silence in our daily life to make progress on the path of finding peace within.

The practice of silence is like a ladder or door which can give us access to inner peace. When we are practising silence, we should be aware of the purpose for which we are practising the silence. Suppression is not silence. The best way to practise silence in our daily life is to watch our reactions. Many times, it's not necessary to react. There are times when only one sentence will suffice, but we go on and on. We want to explain even though all we need to say is 'yes' or 'no.'

Once we realize the role silence can play in experiencing peace, we will be watchful and economical in our words.

What do we do when we are silent? We can practise gratitude. To be grateful for being born as human beings with the potential to be fully self-realized. Being thankful to nature, God or whosoever we believe in for providing us sustenance; being grateful to parents for their love, care, and upbringing; being grateful to our family and friends for bringing light into our lives for there are millions who live a lonely life; being thankful that we have food on our tables and a roof over our heads for, there are millions who go hungry and are homeless in the world. We can use every silent moment to practise gratitude.

Through the practice of silence in our daily life, we can fill our inner space with peace and harmony for us to enjoy and share with our fellow beings.

TRUTH

We need to remain awake all the time because we never know when we will meet the truth face-to-face.

PROBLEMS

Problems look bigger when we think about them; they become smaller when we do something about them.

PEACE

Peace is not the same as feeling good, although feeling good is not bad; peace is the experience of wholeness, the experience of nothing missing.

PRIORITIES

There always is something vying for our attention;
remaining steadfast on our priorities is what turns
out to be beneficial for us and beneficial for others.

PRESENT

Learning to be in the present is like learning to dive in
the water; the more we think, the less likely we will dive.

CHOICE

Every choice involves uncertainty, and yet, we must
make it as life is a series of choices; if we don't,
someone else or something else will make it for us.

ONENESS: LIVE AND LET LIVE

The common thread that runs through all beings is change.

Constant change is the level playing field of existence. No one and nothing is immune from the law of change. Living life from this simple truth can make a profound difference to the way we live our life.

We, human beings have the notion that we are superior species. There is nothing wrong if we consider ourselves as trailblazers for experimentation and innovation, but to think that the human beings have the right to undermine the interests and existence of other species of the planet Earth for the sole benefit of the human race leads to an imbalance in the natural order of things. We don't have to go far to see how this human selfishness has put the very well-being of our planet in jeopardy, disregard of the environment, rampant consumerism, cruelty against animals, destruction of wildlife, and violence are just a few examples.

When we realize that we too are subject to the same law of change that governs the rest of species of this planet, that the wheel of existence moves the same way for the whole creation, it may be possible to puncture human pride and arrogance. Then there is a possibility of humility and humbleness gaining ground in us, and that would be good for the human race. Experiencing oneness will pave the way for genuine "live and let live" not only among fellow human beings but the creation as a whole.

CONTEXT

We may know a lot; however, for our interactions
with people to be productive, we must say
what is necessary for the context.

MIND & BODY

When we slow down our bodily movements,
our mind slows down too; it's a simpler
way to calm down our racing mind.

REASONS

Asking "Why am I doing what I am doing?" is
important because things are unlikely to work
out if we do them for the wrong reasons.

PAUSE

One must pause, take some time before one
agrees or disagrees, as the right questions
surface only in the light of looking.

SUFFERING

Trying to escape from suffering is futile;
the mind goes where we go.

PAST

The past is always relevant, not to live but to learn from.

POWER AND RESPONSIBILITY

Gautama, the Buddha said, "You are your own master; you make your own future."

To realize that one is one's master changes the whole paradigm of life and the way one is living. It brings forth power and responsibility, power to choose and responsibility to act according to one's choices.

Only we can decide whether our career choice is right, whether the relationships we have are nurturing, the hobbies we pursue are making us happy, beliefs whether spiritual, social, political or mundane are taking us in the right direction.

When we wake up to who we are, living becomes meaningful. One needs to turn inward and introspect. Introspection is not brooding or indulging in self-pity and blame. It's to take an honest look at oneself and accept what comes up rather than resist or deny. Unconditional acceptance of what is not working is the first step towards finding what could work.

To make changes or take a new direction is not easy. One is often weighed down by the word responsibility. However, if we wake up to our power and potential that comes from realizing that each one of us is indeed one's master, it may not seem so daunting. It may give rise to a new purpose and new dreams.

LONGEVITY

It doesn't matter so much whether life is long
or short; what matters is whether we are aware,
it's happening moment by moment.

LET GO

Hard it is to let go, but harder still is to let
go of something that has already left.

SELF-COMPASSION

Trying to develop compassion for others
before we have developed self-compassion is
like putting the cart before the horse.

EQUANIMITY

We should be grateful that there often is
something missing in our lives for those are
the moments to cultivate equanimity.

FREEDOM

Harder the truth hits, deeper is an experience of freedom.

TOLERANCE

Never deny others' experience for "only the
wearer knows where the shoe pinches."

POSSIBILITY OF A NEW YEAR

There is a difference between "already knowing" and "knowing." Former offers us false security and comfort but robs us of aliveness. The latter is more challenging but comes with a possibility of life being an adventure. We can call "already knowing" assumptions as well.

A New Year is an opportunity to reflect and inquire into our assumptions and how this way of being is stopping us from experiencing newness and creating new possibilities in our life.

For example, maybe:

- The person we wanted to communicate with, but didn't, would understand our communication.

- It's possible to get up early in the morning and enjoy the sunrise.

- I am not as lazy as I think to start to go to the gym or to jog.

- My assumption that my spouse, my family will never understand me is fallacious.

- Spirituality and meditation are not for old age alone.

- It's never too late to tread a new path.

- The government is doing something right.

- The society is not as unjust as we think.

- There is more good than evil in the world.

- It is possible for me and others to change.

We can go on, but each one of us will know their assumptions better.

Assumptions solidify a reality, whereas the reality is malleable and adaptable. When we turn the beam of attention on our assumptions, they begin to melt. Assumptions do not allow us to experiment and keep us in the same groove. Looking into and examining our assumptions can create a possibility of finding new ways of relating to the self and others.

When we let go of our assumptions, we create choices. Living life with choices is aliveness and freedom.

A NEW BEGINNING

Completions create new possibilities of living; incompletions put us in the hold mode in life.

It may sound unbelievable, but it's true that sometimes the incompletion we have been hanging on to for years may require only a phone call to complete. It is not uncommon to hear people make a total break with the past because it was not fulfilling for them. While it's never too late to make a new beginning in our relationships, work situations, personal preferences, interests or hobbies, we can avoid the suffering we go through in the process if we make a habit of not accumulating incompletions.

If it happens, it's great, but usually, completions don't happen by chance. It is an intentional action.

Every action repeated over a period becomes a habit. Similarly, every inaction repeated over a period also becomes a habit. The inaction as regards to incompletions is no exception. It creates a comfort zone that we don't like to step out, and get resigned and used to. Gradually, the resignation begins to make a dent in our aliveness and freedom of expression, which is the cost we pay when we don't proactively try to eliminate incompletions from our life.

What are some of the personal and interpersonal areas where incompletions show up?

"Procrastination is the thief of time." We have heard this before, but the cost of procrastination is more than the loss of time. It erodes our self-esteem as we begin to lose confidence in getting things done on time and in a nice way. Procrastination and resultant incompletions feed each other and create a vicious circle, which is difficult to break unless we stir ourselves into action.

Relationships are the main area where incompletions rear their not-so-pretty face. The two most essential ingredients of healthy relationships are mutual respect and trust. When we sacrifice openness and honesty in relationships and let the incompletions build up, we lose out on mutual respect and trust. Then we can have only surface-level relationships, which is not bad, but it is a far cry from creating empowering long-term relationships.

So, it may be a good idea for us to pick up the phone and make the call we wanted to make for a long time, and we don't have to wait for the new year to make a new beginning!

GRATITUDE

When we start our day with the feelings
of gratitude, every day is a new day!

FAITH

Faith is not hoping for the best; it is that power which
keeps us going when we have reached the end of the road.

SPREAD THE LIGHT

It is natural to feel good if someone makes
our day. However, it would be great if that
inspires us to make someone else's day.

PATIENCE

The more attached we are, the less patience we have.

TIMING

What one wants to do may be good and in one's interests. However, it may be worthwhile to run a reality check on the timing before we act upon it.

VIGILANCE

Peace of mind is a beautiful but very fragile state of mind. It can only be sustained through constant vigilance.

DILEMMA: AN OPPORTUNITY

"Do you have the patience to wait till your mud settles
and the water is clear? Can you remain unmoving
till the right action emerges by itself?" – Lao Tzu

A dilemma is an opportunity to get in touch with one's
vision. It's similar to choice-making, but more prolonged
and uncomfortable because pros and cons seem to be evenly
balanced. If we try to force our way through a dilemma,
the results are not very satisfactory. Finding a way through
dilemma is a process. It's more like watching the situation
as an observer and letting the right choice emerge.

As one is going through the process, there are two things
to reflect upon:

Firstly, how would the given options affect our well-being
and the well-being of those who are close to us? Is the option
we are leaning towards inspiring? Is it worth our time and
energy?

The second point to consider is whether what we want to embark upon is consistent with our vision and how taking it on would impact our existing goals and future planning. Let's not go too far in the future.

Now, we should allow time for options to play out and present their case to us. It is natural that sometimes we will lean towards one option and sometimes towards the other, but with patience, we will find clarity dawn on us, and we will start seeing the light at the end of the tunnel.

While there is no harm in discussing and taking suggestions from others, one who is in the midst of a dilemma will alone know what is important to him or her. If we have patiently gone through the process, sooner or later, a clear choice will emerge that will untangle the dilemma.

The time and energy spent while going through this process is never wasted. We will gain more clarity on what is important to us. We will either reset our priorities or stick to our current priorities with more conviction and greater certainty. In either case, we will feel empowered to forge ahead.

LIVING A CHOICE

There is a world of difference between making a choice and living it. It's like making a selection from a menu and eating the meal; the two are entirely different experiences.

When our choice turns out to be right, we feel elated. It sends pleasant vibrations through our body. We and possibly others give us a pat on the back. We are the smartest people out there.

When our choice turns out to be wrong, we feel bad. We experience unpleasant feelings and look out for the exit door or try to find a scapegoat or feel guilty.

We realize the negative side of our good choice and positive side of our bad choice as we begin to live with our choices irrespective of whether it's a major choice or the choices we make in our daily life on a continuous basis. We forget quite easily that every coin has two sides.

Every choice is a mix of good and bad. When we accept and practise this in our daily life, we will be better prepared to deal with the unexpected consequences and feelings that surface after we have made a choice.

CHOICE

Every day, we have a choice to relive the complaints
and resentments of yesterday, or, forgive and let
go to lay the foundation for a better tomorrow.

OBJECTIVITY

When we take ourselves out of the equation,
options begin to emerge effortlessly.

TRANSFORMATION

Transformation is an inside job that is
best done in the outside world.

INSIGHTS

Insights, though valuable, are not sufficient
to bring about change. Insights must inspire
our daily living to be meaningful.

SING A SONG!

Both, positive and the negative, are interpretations;
however, one sings a new song every day, every moment,
whereas, the other keeps playing the same old tune
again and again: I am right, others are wrong.

BACKBONE

Moral conduct is the backbone of who we are. We often
get caught up in the shortcuts and neglect our backbone.

TIMELINE

Timelines when used constructively bring out the best in us. They create a commitment to achieve goals. We can prioritize and organize our work schedule, delegate, track progress and make changes if necessary as we execute our plans.

However, quite often, after we have met a timeline, there is a feeling that we've missed out some essential element or we could have improved upon the result. We quickly forget that in hindsight, everything can be done much better.

The need for perfection and meeting timelines go ill together. The die-hard perfectionists are never quite ready because even their best is not good enough! A perfectionist always holds out for something better with the result that deadlines get extended, and when met, they bring in their wake much stress and anxiety. It's like chasing a mirage.

Producing results is an art of the possible, not perfection. We learn as long as we live. If we let go of our need to be a perfectionist, we can be effective as well as have a sense of satisfaction in our lives.

APPRECIATION

Everything passes away; what remains are the
memories of appreciation and acknowledgment.

AWAKENING

You don't need to get the murmurs of self-awakening
validated externally; no one can hear them except you.

PEOPLE

If we look at the gold ornaments, variety will baffle
us; when we look at the gold, they are all the same.

EXPECTATIONS

Expectations, when fulfilled, give short-term satisfaction; expectations, when not fulfilled, leave long-term frustrations.

REFLECTION

If we take a moment to reflect before we say or do something, we may find that quite a few things we want to say or do are not necessary.

MIND & BODY

When we do one thing at a time, our mind and body are connected.

MOODS

Generally speaking, "moods" have a negative connotation. We all have moods. Some of us are good at controlling our moods, whereas their moods control some. If we are suppressing our moods, that too is not a good way of handling them as they are likely to erupt when we least expect them.

We find it difficult to handle our moods because we consider "being moody" as part of one's nature. This approach only leaves us helpless in the face of moods. It need not be that way.

Consider moods as passing clouds, and you'll have the true nature of moods. Clouds come in different shapes and sizes, some dense and heavy, others thin and light, but they all pass away. Similarly, how so ever gloomy or sad a mood may be, it invariably passes away.

Moods are the mind's way to overpower us. The mind operates through our senses. Any trigger is good enough to change our mood: what we see, hear, smell, taste, touch and think is capable of changing and does change our mood to lesser or greater degree, except that we are not fully aware that change is occurring.

The pre-requisite of handling our moods is awareness. Once we are aware that a mood change is setting in or has already set in, the best way to handle it is to do nothing, except "to be" with it, observe it, and remind ourselves that it's a passing phenomenon.

Gradually, as we begin to see the true nature of moods, we will become more aware of when we find ourselves in one of the moods. Then we can smile and say, "I know who you are, a passing cloud."

IDEA

It's not good to write off any idea lightly, for
the secrets of success are often hidden in
the pages of what has been written off.

GOODNESS

If you want to know how good a person would
be a mother, father, husband, wife, friend, or for
that matter, **the leader of a nation,** then look
at how good he or she is as a human being.

HAPPINESS

Not everyone can climb Mt Everest, not everyone can
become rich and famous, but it's possible for everyone
to be happy if we let go of our need to be somebody.

THOUGHTS

As trimming and watering without good seed cannot
make a healthy tree, deeds and words without good
thoughts cannot make a healthy human being.

SADNESS

Sadness is a sublime emotion to get soaked
into rather than be ashamed of.

GREATNESS

The best way to feel great is to see greatness in others.

TRAINING THE MIND

The mind is like a monkey - not just any monkey but the drunken monkey, ceaselessly leaping from one thought to another. While that is true, we have also heard about the possibility of making our mind an instrument of peace, happiness, power, and contribution. Is this possible or is this wishful thinking?

If we look closely, it will become obvious that even this monkey mind gets a lot of things done for us. Our daily routine, job responsibilities, household functions, etc., they all get accomplished with the help of our mind. The problem is that the mind does all these things mechanically, the way it knows best. It reacts the way it has always reacted. It is always in auto mode. Our likes, dislikes, preferences, pretty much everything is preconditioned. As a result, we don't experience aliveness in our relationships; there is no newness or freshness in the way we experience our world. We don't even see the possibility of our world expanding beyond our mundane existence. Is it possible to train our mind to see that possibility?

"But we are so comfortable the way we are, why do we have to look beyond our mundane existence?" We need to look beyond mundane life because the persistent feeling of unease and unsatisfactoriness we experience underneath the comfort of our worldly life will never go away unless we address it. Ignorance can never give us the experience of bliss; it only numbs our mind.

When we want to keep ourselves physically fit and keep our body in good shape, we exercise, walk, jog, swim, go to the gym, learn yoga, tai chi, and do several other things. We take a lot of effort if we are serious and we have no problem with making these efforts. It is no different when it comes to the mind. If we have allowed our mind to become gross, it is reasonable to say that we are the ones who have to make it subtle and healthy so that we may experience aliveness and newness.

Our mind does help us in attending to our daily tasks reasonably well. It follows that our mind is amenable to training. If we can train our mind to do mundane jobs, we can very well train it to look beyond mundane life because that is where the true joy of life lies.

To accomplish anything - whether mundane or spiritual - we need to develop concentration. We can do with less concentration to perform our daily, repetitive activities. We need deeper concentration and strong determination to train our mind to abandon its waywardness and become an effective instrument for experiencing peace and joy of living.

It's no different from going to the gym to strengthen our body. Meditation, mindfulness, and contemplation are some of the tools to make our mind subtle and healthy.

NEW DAY

Our mind and body try to tell us a new story every
day; listening to that story, particularly in the
morning, is what makes every day **a new day!**

BLESSINGS

To count one's blessings is great. But it's more important
to develop compassion for those who are less blessed.

POSSIBILITY

The nature of a possibility is such that it keeps
expanding when we take the first step; all we
need is a little courage and a lot of faith.

EFFORTS

Sincere efforts have magic to turn a
journey into a destination.

EGO

Ego takes many disguises to hide the simple truth that
we suffer because we neglect to do the right thing.

TRUTH

Allow yourself to experience your truth; no one
in the world knows it better than you do.

HOW TO THINK AND BE POSITIVE

"We are shaped by our thoughts; we become
what we think." – The Buddha

When our mind is filled with anger; we become angry; when greed takes control of our mind; we become greedy; when our mind is gross and deluded, we become gross and deluded.

We are loving, compassionate, and generous when there are thoughts of love, compassion, and generosity in our mind.

Also, we have to realize it very deeply that when we create negativities in our mind, we become their first victims; and the reverse too is equally valid. When we develop thoughts of love, compassion, and kindness, we experience peace and happiness. Unless we see the cost we are paying - both physical and mental - when we create defilements, the shift from negative to positive will be short-lived.

Now, since we know we become what we think, we have to think what we want to become.

We see anger and ill-will rising in our mind; we can remind ourselves of the cost we are paying by harbouring ill-will and hatred. Whether or not it's going to harm another person, we know it's damaging us for sure. Also, we can remind ourselves that everyone is on their journey. We don't know how life has treated others. This way, we are replacing thoughts of ill-will and animosity with the thoughts of understanding and kindness.

When we see greed, lust, and craving rising in our mind, we can remind ourselves of their transitory nature, and the truth that craving will lead to more craving and greed will lead to more greed. Succumbing to greed and lust has its cost. This way, we are replacing unwholesome thoughts of greed, craving, and lust with the thoughts of equanimity and renunciation.

We see confusion and doubts rising in our mind; we can remind ourselves that confusion and doubts are normal in the quest for knowledge, and with patience and forbearance, they will give place to faith and trust. This way, we are replacing thoughts of ignorance and skepticism with the thoughts of patience and wisdom.

The transformation from positive to negative is a gradual process, and it requires serious work. When we work at the root level of the mind, it takes more time and work, but the results are more profound and penetrate everyday life.

POSITIVE & NEGATIVE

Negative sees only negative; positive sees both negative
and positive, then decides positive is a better option.

PEOPLE

We feel more connected and respect people more
when we consider them a resource to learn from.

WORDS

Human beings were designed more for silence;
words are the invention of the human mind;
the less we use, the better off we will be.

VARIETY

If you are happy with what you are doing or having, don't change it; happiness is more important than variety.

HATRED

Hatred hides the deep sorrow within.

MOVING ON

Never ignore the shoulder that is waiting to be leaned on; maybe leaning on it is what will help you to move on.

STILLNESS

The mind will never be completely still until one has attained nirvana, which is beyond the reach of most of us. Still, we should work towards that goal as we are fortunate to have this precious human birth. Until we have reached that stage, however, we have to deal with our mind and its restlessness.

Our mind is multitasking all the time. It tries to think of different things at the same time. It wouldn't be a problem if we were aware of it and observed its working, but most of the time it succeeds in taking away our attention, and we start swaying with it. When we do this, it has successfully transferred its restlessness to us.

On the other hand, we, as an observer or witness, can distance ourselves from the restlessness of the mind and remain detached observing our changing thoughts.

Observing is not analyzing. It is watching the flow of thoughts without unconsciously getting drawn into them.

Something like watching the ebb and flow of the tide without getting wet.

Doubt may arise that if we just keep watching our thoughts then how we will manage our daily life?

We are less effective and take a longer time to take decisions or to make up our mind when we are being pulled and pushed by the conflicting thoughts. When we are aware of and watching our thoughts, they cannot overpower us; they slow down. The stillness that follows will make us more alert and effective. In the light of awareness, we will be able to manage our lives more efficiently and feel less stressed at the end of the day.

WHY MEDITATE?

Meditation is an art of being in the present.

The main point to notice in our everyday experience is that the mind constantly wanders. That it wanders away to good, bad or ugly, though important, is a secondary issue.

The mind is like any other tool. If we want to work with a tool, we should know how to use it effectively. We are often reminded to be positive. While one can hardly question the wisdom of this advice, it's possible to develop and sustain such attitude only when we have trained our mind to remain still to some extent.

We experience peace and aliveness when we are in the present moment, whereas the mind relishes remaining in the past or the future. One could say, "In that case, let's ignore the mind." We cannot ignore the mind for the simple reason that the mind is all we have. Either we constructively use its power, or we let it drag us in its wanderlust.

Meditation can help us rein the waywardness of our mind. Even momentary stillness can make a big difference in how we feel and how we deal with challenges in our daily life. Having seen the purpose of meditation, how do we go about it?

While determination and commitment are necessary, we need to know a proper technique. Having learned the correct technique, one must practise it daily over a period. If the technique is correct, one would see some results right away, but long-lasting results will come when meditation is practised consistently over a period.

As with any other skill, it takes the time to learn and achieve reasonable proficiency in meditation. In meditation, there are no shortcuts. It's not something one learns through reading, listening, thinking, watching or talking. They help, but progress is possible only through sustained practice.

The litmus test of any meditation technique is whether it's helping us slow down our monkey mind, helping us to slow down our reactions while being alert internally. The change should be visible and experienced in our daily life. We don't become less efficient or less productive when our reactions slow down. On the contrary, our actions become less abrupt and more thoughtful. We react less and respond more.

Regular practice of meditation can make us calm and peaceful, and at the same time paves the way for purifying negativities.

MINDFULNESS

Every moment we have an opportunity to abide in real, in the present. It is the essence of mindfulness. No matter how long we have been daydreaming, we can always come back to the present moment - from unreal to real.

When we are aware of what we see with our eyes, hearing with our ears, tasting with our tongue, smelling with our nose, feeling with our body, and are aware of the thoughts that are going through our mind, we are practising mindfulness.

Meditation and mindfulness complement each other. Meditation helps us to be mindful in our daily life; mindfulness helps us to deepen our meditation.

Mindfulness, apart from making us more effective and alert in our mundane activities, also makes us calm and peaceful because when we are mindful, our mind is not racing, and even if it does, we can slow it down.

Walk when walking, sit when sitting, eat when eating..., this is the highest peace.

ROUTINE

Routine is neither exciting nor boring; what we do
in the routine makes it interesting or boring.

VISUALIZATION

To shake off the lethargy, visualize how
you will feel after you get going!

FEAR

It's not possible to see things clearly when
we are in the grip of fear; fear does to our
consciousness what stone does to still water.

INTERACTION

Every interaction is an opportunity to
make or mar someone's day.

GOODWILL

The compulsion to prove oneself ceases,
when our actions spring from goodwill.

WRONGDOING

It's no shame to be ashamed of
wrongdoing; it's right awareness.

PARENTING

The best gift we can give to our children is
to help them discover their potential.

PARENTING–I

INCULCATING MINDFULNESS IN CHILDREN

It's never too late to inculcate mindfulness in children, but early age is the best time to make a beginning. At an early age, children are open and eager to learn as they are not set in their ways. The lessons they learn and the habits they form at an early age influence them throughout life.

Mindfulness is a wider subject that can include watching our actions, bodily sensations, feelings, thoughts, etc. However, the focus here is the first lesson in mindfulness practice: learning to do "one thing at a time," and that too in the context of children. Let's take a few examples from our daily life:

It's very common to try diverting children's attention to feed them or getting them to perform a minor task. To start with, it may sound like a clever tactic, but in the long run, it doesn't help the children to learn to focus as they get used to distractions. What happens next? When the children are ready to eat by themselves, they want a toy to play with while eating. When they are ready to dress, they want to watch TV. Regardless of our intentions, we have habituated them to do one thing while paying attention to another.

Parents have a golden opportunity to plant a seed of mindfulness in their children at an early age. As children are very impressionable at this age, it will not take much time for the seed to grow if watered with patience, persistence, love, and firmness. Interestingly, we don't have to use the word mindfulness, but that is what they will be learning if we apply "one thing at a time" principle.

Mindfulness is one of the basic building blocks of character and doing "one thing at a time" its first lesson. Parents can give a head start to their children by teaching this simple habit to them.

Sure, there will be challenges along the way, but if we think ahead, we can easily see that the benefits far outweigh the work we have to put in:

- Once "one thing at a time" becomes a habit, the children will be able to accomplish basic tasks like eating, dressing themselves, making their bed, etc. independently and in less time - a big relief for parents.

- The children will be able to concentrate better, and the results will show up in their studies and extra-curricular activities.

- The children will develop good listening skills, a critical ingredient of learning.

- With listening comes understanding, with understanding comes appreciation.

- Mindful children will grow to become mindful adults. There are better chances of them not only excelling in their chosen pursuits but also in living life fully.

The children may not remember us for the material things we provide them, but they will remember us for the feeling that we cherished them and for the good habits we helped them to learn.

PARENTING–II
NEVER LET YOUR DREAMS DIE

Chasing dreams based on others' expectations can never give us a sense of fulfillment. Parents try to project their expectations on their children. The whole conversation around us, while we are growing up, is about "becoming." Survival, not the fulfillment, is the guiding principle. Gradually, we begin to internalize others' expectations and believe them to be our dreams.

This doesn't mean there are no self-generated dreams. There are self-generated dreams, but we need to distinguish the ends from the means to appreciate them.

A dream to care for sick and the infirm need not die if I fail to become a doctor. A dream to help provide housing for homeless need not fall apart if I fail to become an engineer or architect. A dream of elevating poverty and serve my people need not vanish if I fail to win elections or fail to become a minister or a secretary. A dream of leaving behind a legacy for my family or community need not weaken just because I haven't amassed great wealth. In all these examples, one is a dream and the other just a means to realize a dream. We can always try a different means to realize our dreams.

If we make this distinction and choose a dream that inspires us, setbacks will not make us give up on our dream. We may feel a little disappointed if we fail at a particular endeavour, but the fire in our dreams will lead us to new beginnings.

What we do and believe is, to a great extent, the function of the conversation and expectations around us in the family and the cues we get from society. If there is a conversation of success interspersed with the conversation of contribution and giving in the family, it is very likely that a child will grow up imbibing these values, and they will show up in what he or she does later in life. If there is a conversation of equanimity and contentment side by side with the talk of dreaming big, a child will have a better chance of remaining centred in good and bad times, to remain steadfast in the direction of their dreams under challenging circumstances.

Nowadays, it's heartening to see young parents giving more time and attention to their children and their development. However, the attention is mostly on the physical and mental development. Getting them interested in studies, games, and other activities at a young age is good. At the same time, if they are encouraged to take an interest in spiritual development as well, their progress will be balanced and well-rounded. They will be better equipped to handle the vicissitudes of life.

POTENTIAL

If we look at what others do, we may miss out
on our potential; but if we pay attention to how
passionately others are doing what they are
doing, we may discover our own potential.

NEED & GREED

Greed is in mind; the body just has needs.

CHANGE THYSELF

We cannot change other people; only they can
change themselves. In the same way, no one
else can change us but ourselves, and yet we
try to change other people all the time.

TIME

When we do what needs to be done right now,
we are free from the bondage of time.

GENEROSITY

We see the generosity of others after they have
become generous, but expect others to see our
generosity before we have become generous.

MINDFUL

Being mindful is to be respectful to
the object of our attention.

BREAKDOWNS:

AN OPPORTUNITY FOR RENEWAL

Breakdowns are an opportunity to rest and rejuvenate - the same as we take the exit for a rest area before resuming a long drive.

Project breakdowns can be an opportunity to reflect upon our assumptions: completion timeline, workforce requirements, financial resources, a shift in the market demand and so forth.

The breakdown in the achievement of goals, either personal or professional, is an opportunity to take a fresh look at the challenges: Where has my motivation gone? Maybe I have to rekindle my dreams and get inspired! Have I overreached myself? Have I too much on my plate? Maybe, I have to slow down and take the much-needed break.

A breakdown in health can prove to be a blessing in disguise if we use this opportunity to make some necessary lifestyle changes, for instance, to set up an exercise routine, learn yoga, go for a morning or evening walk, consume less caffeine, make diet changes, eat at regular times, schedule regular medical check-ups, etc. It's not uncommon for people to give up unhealthy habits like smoking and drinking after a health breakdown.

A breakdown, or a lack of warmth in a relationship, need not be a cause for self-pity or blame game. Instead, it could reignite the fire in a relationship. All we have to do here is to do some honest introspection and give some rest to our ego.

The "something is missing" feeling can be a wonderful opportunity to turn inward and find the riches that lie within us.

The knot that hinders breakdowns from turning into breakthroughs is our over-emphasis and preoccupation with finding faults in others before we get into action. Fault finding has its place, but it's not pre-requisite for doing what is needed to be done to get things moving again. When we mix up these two, we create a stalemate.

What is required is clarity about our commitments. When we are committed to creating breakthroughs, we will not allow reasons to come in the way. If our commitment is to find faults, breakdowns will not only persist but deepen. It's our choice.

More often than not, breakdowns are caused by minor issues that get magnified out of proportion with the passage of time, and we get resigned to a situation or a problem, be it concerning our dreams, relationships, health, career or any other matter. Seeing the big picture can help us make the right choice. It's not worth sacrificing our cherished goals, relationships, our health and happiness for the sake of issues that will not matter in the long run.

PURPOSE OF LIFE

Avoid what is unnecessary; do what is necessary.
What advances the purpose of our life is
necessary; what doesn't is unnecessary.

INSPIRED LIVING

Our living becomes inspired when we
see meaning in everyday life.

PATIENCE

From time to time, we feel overwhelmed by the
circumstances and try to force our way out. It
doesn't work that way. We need the patience
most when we have reached the end of it.

KARMAS

Remembering that we meet people and part ways for a reason, takes the sting out of our regrets and complaints.

PROBLEMS

It's not the problem, but the shadow of the problem, that robs us of peace of mind.

HAPPINESS

We have a choice to be happy or unhappy. When we choose to remain equanimous in the face of ups and downs of life, we have cast our vote in favour of being happy.

IT'S A NEW DAY

Every morning when we wake up, it's a new day, the first day of our life. A bit overused, but true. When we wake up in the morning, we go about our business as usual not realizing that this is the first day of our life, and this could be the last day because the truth is, we go to bed at night without any assurance that we will wake up in the morning. Seeing this simple truth and making it a part of our daily experience can change our approach to life.

Sometimes the truth is so obvious that we don't see it, the same as when an object is too close to our eyes we can't see it. When we don't see the obvious, we miss out on the possibilities lying hidden.

When we are visiting a place, say a historical city, resort, a beach, a museum and have a day to spend, we try to see as much as possible and enjoy every moment for we don't know whether we will return to that place again. It is the same with life when we truly believe that this day is probably the only one we have to live. Then we will live life to the fullest.

All quarrels will end. It's inconceivable that one would harbour animosity or ill-will against anyone on one's last day.

It would seem pointless to accumulate things beyond one's necessities. Greed would give way to need; competition to cooperation; selfishness to sharing and generosity. One would express love more readily than withhold it. We would smile and laugh more. The possibilities are endless.

We find it difficult to reconcile with the inevitability and uncertainty of death. Much of this unease will go away because now we would know that this could be our last day and tomorrow we will be born again, as the Buddha said, "Every morning we are born again. What we do today is what matters most."

CONTRIBUTION

When we see others' contribution from our point of view, we see only shortcomings; when we let go of our point of view, it begins to make sense.

RESPECT

Believe in yourself and say what you believe in. This is the best way to be respected.

MATURITY

Silence, not the words; restraint, not the reaction, is a pathway to maturity.

ARROGANCE

All sufferings are painful, but the suffering
of arrogance is most painful.

WAY

There is no other way except to find one's own way.

JOY

What kills the joy of living is our compulsion
to reach somewhere; how wonderful it would
be to discover we are where we need to be.

LIVE LIFE IN YOUR LIGHTS

We are all influenced in greater or lesser degree by the opinions of others. However, when getting approval from others becomes our need, it limits us, it takes away our freedom.

How does need for approval limit us:

1. We are afraid or hesitant to express our point of view. This limits our expression.
2. It comes in the way of building or deepening relationships as we don't open our heart and express our sincere feelings lest we step on someone's toes.
3. We can lose bigger opportunities as we are afraid to go beyond our comfort zone.
4. It makes a dent in our self-esteem as we know we are not true to ourselves and not living to our potential.
5. Others too, sooner or later, find out that we are not being honest, and may not take us seriously.

6. Our desire to please others will keep us stressed as we are always trying to figure out what the other person wants to hear.

7. We may be spending too much time, and energy on what we think may please others rather than concentrating on what is important to us.

How do we come out of, or minimize, our need for approval?

1. Decide what is important to you. Once you find out what is important to you and you enjoy doing it, you will be less concerned about others' acceptance of what you are doing.

2. People are still relevant, but not their approval. Always remember "there never is, never was and never will be a person who was only appreciated or only blamed." The Buddha

3. Don't confuse appreciation with approval. Appreciation is a beautiful face of human nature. It's a blessing. One doesn't seek appreciation, but when it is shown, both the giver and the receiver are united in the bond of respect and gratitude.

4. Having self-approved, dedicate yourself to the objective with all commitment and sincerity.

Our mind will still try to search for outside approval. When it does, just say, "I know better."

ECHO

Harsh words hurt; but not as much
as the echo of harsh words.

PATIENCE

Patience is a wonderful remedy; it cures all ills.

SOLITUDE

When we learn to enjoy our own
company, we are never bored.

RIGHT

Stay close to what you think is right. We may not conquer the world, but we will be at peace, and that may well turn out to be more important than conquering the world.

BE YOURSELF

People are easily impressed when we connect with them; it's hard to connect when we try to impress them.

ACCEPTANCE

If we don't like something that has been hanging around in our life for a long time in spite of our best efforts, just accept it; it might be waiting for a fitting farewell before it leaves.

KEEPING OUR WORD

Keeping word is an act of faith, especially when the outcome is uncertain. We start with small things in our daily life, which may seem inconsequential, but by doing what we have promised, we make a habit of keeping our word. This is an interim stage.

The real test is when it comes to keeping our word to ourselves. Since nobody is watching and no one will turn back to remind or point the finger at us, it's easier to get away by not keeping a promise to oneself.

When we don't keep our word to others, it makes a dent in our credibility. People may stop taking us seriously. When we don't keep our word to ourselves, it erodes our self-esteem, and we feel less confident of acting on our intentions.

When we keep our word, it frees us - one less thing to do. When we don't keep our word, it adds to our burden which keeps accumulating. It may appear that we have got used to the burden, but we realize how heavy it was when we take it off.

WRONG

Wrong does not become right just because
an alternative is not in sight.

PROGRESS

Progress from one point to another is
possible only on the wheels of change.

MIRACLE

That we keep breathing without a break is in itself a
miracle; we shouldn't be surprised when the miracle ends.

LEARNING

Learning never ends, but the source of learning
keeps changing: from external to internal.

KNOWLEDGE

To know more is not knowledge, to
know right is knowledge.

PEOPLE

People become a problem when we try to decide
for them, on the other hand, they become an
asset when we let them decide for themselves.

SELF-RESTRAINT

The thought is the mother of all we say and do, except that in most part, we are not watchful of our thoughts. The result is, we often say words that are better left unsaid, and take actions that are better left alone. To expect that we will never make mistakes as regards to what we say or do would be unrealistic, but we can minimize the possibility of saying and doing things we might regret later.

The first step is to watch our thoughts constantly. Thoughts should be converted into words or actions only after we have screened them. We are not counting emergencies here when our body and mind operate from the basic instinct of survival.

As we begin to observe our thoughts, we will find that we are better able to restrain ourselves from saying and doing things that are not necessary, but we keep saying and doing them. As we go along deepening our practice of being mindful of our thoughts, our experience of daily life starts changing for the better. We will have fewer reasons to regret, and more reasons to feel good as our newly-acquired ability to control our impulses and reactions would boost our self-confidence and improve our self-esteem.

Self-restraint is not the same as self-suppression. In self-suppression, we stop the thinking process, whereas self-restraint is the result of the thoughtful application of mind.

Self-restraint helps, not hinders self-expression. Both can go together. We can learn valuable lessons in how to be appropriate with people by exercising self-restraint. When we are appropriate, our interactions with people are smooth and frictionless. We have a feeling of being in harmony with our world. Self-restraint, when practised with conviction, is beneficial to us as well as others.

TRUST

It would be impossible to live our normal life without trusting that people will follow the rules. We walk worry-free on the pavements because we believe motorists will observe traffic rules. We shop in malls believing shop owners will respect our decision if we choose not to buy from their stores. We travel in buses, trains, and fly in airplanes trusting the skills of drivers and pilots to arrive safely at the destination. Accidents and unusual occurrences do happen, but generally, normal life flows smoothly from day to day.

However, when it comes to personal, business, and social life, it's not so straightforward. We tend to trust or distrust people through the lenses of our likes and dislikes. Impressions and feelings play a significant role in our decisions to trust or distrust people. The impressions and feelings, likes and dislikes are unfortunately not very reliable pointers and, more often than not, lead to wrong conclusions.

Trust is a function of understanding, and it comes through communication rather than confrontation or keeping things vague. However, not every communication leads to understanding. We can talk and talk, and yet, may not be wiser at the end of the day. Intention and sincerity play a significant role in the process. If we stick to our agenda, it may not work out satisfactorily for us or others. Although, we should not compromise on gaining clarity, persuasion and respect for one another can achieve better results than arguments or unwillingness to engage in dialogue. As communication moves from superficial to relevant, confusion gives place to clarity and clarity to understanding. With understanding, trust comes easily and effortlessly.

It may also be useful to look at what allows people to trust us. Simply put, when we do what we say, not occasionally, but consistently, then people begin to trust and respect us. People may be impressed by our words, but they will believe us only by our deeds. Besides, we are less likely to go wrong with people if we pay more attention to what they do rather than what they say.

SPONTANEITY

Freedom, not speed, is the real measure of spontaneity.

GRUDGES

Agree to disagree is the best way to
give grudges time to heal.

BEST FOOT FORWARD

It is possible to put our "best foot forward,"
when it is placed on the land of truth.

ANONYMITY

If my name disappears after I disappear, I don't get to
see the fun; joy is in the experience of anonymity.

RESULTS

We have no control over the results. However, if we follow
through what we consider the right thing to do, we will be
fine if it happens, and we will be fine if it doesn't happen.

REDISCOVERY

Life will never become monotonous if
we keep rediscovering ourselves.

GENUINE INSPIRATION

Much as we would like and hope, inspiration does not fall from the sky. It is not a feeling that comes and goes. Genuine inspiration is an act of creation, the result of focused attention on an issue that is important to us. It's the outcome of the continued application of mind on the issue that we want to untangle or the goal we want to achieve but somehow don't see a way through it.

For instance, I want to paint. Most of us would consider this activity as one of a pure act of inspiration, almost like something falling in our lap from nowhere. But here also, if I just wait and hope, not much is going to happen. I need to put some thought into it. What kind of a painting do I want to paint? Is it going to be abstract art, figure painting or landscape? Oil or watercolours? Having decided the medium, I may want to do some research in the area. Gradually, the fog surrounding my aspiration will clear, and the picture will become vivid, creating a solid base for meaningful action. Now, I will be able to draw inspiration from every source as

I have done the groundwork and planted the seed. This is a genuine inspiration.

Then what about inspirational speakers, inspirational books, inspirational talks, etc.? They all help. But if all we can say after listening to an inspirational teacher or guru is, "Wow, what a fantastic talk!" and then not do anything, it will serve little purpose. It may give us short-lived, passing inspiration. However, they can stir us into action only when we reflect on their message, relate to it to see how it will pan out in our life situation, our goals, and our dreams.

While there is nothing wrong with looking for inspiration to accelerate attainment of our objectives, finding what our passion and goals are, is something that we alone can do for ourselves. Only we can know and decide what inspires and lights us up. If we look at others to determine what motivates us, we will miss out on our potential.

Genuine inspiration should mobilize our mind and body into concrete action. It should help us shake off lethargy, uncertainty, and self-doubt; and propel us into action. This isn't a one-time job. We must recreate it every time we get stuck, every time we want to ignite the fire in us.

FEAR

Anything done half-heartedly breeds fear of being caught.

MIND

The mind latches on to every hope of becoming. Initially, it looks quite harmless and reasonable until it turns into attachment.

GOALS

The past cannot provide the answers for the future; it can only show us how far we are from our goals and the work we have to do to reach there.

PROCRASTINATION

"I will do it later," gets done when it's too late, if at all.

INTEGRITY

The source of unease is a lack of integrity. It's
hard to see because it makes us look bad.

WISDOM

When someone learns from you, it is their wisdom;
what you learn from them is your wisdom.

WINNING HEARTS

There is no better way to realize the urgency of winning hearts than to quote Jose Ortega y Gasset's famous quote: "We cannot put off living until we are ready. The most salient characteristic of life is its urgency, "here and now" without possible postponement. Life is fired at us point-blank."

These words capture the essence of the dilemma called human existence. This moment is all we have. We cannot wait for the next moment because every next moment will come as "this" moment. We react and repent. In hindsight, we could have done everything much better. But we cannot wait to live, and when we react, often, we find we have hurt people, said things that could have remained unsaid, done things that we could have done better. Then how must one live?

The first thing is to slow down. When we slow down, every moment seems to last longer. Our reactions become more measured and thoughtful, less abrupt. We realize that sometimes just being silent is a more effective way to communicate provided silence is practised with empathy and love, not as 'silent treatment.'

The second thing is to realize that in life, those who lose happily and smilingly are the ones who emerge winners. Winning arguments and scoring points are easy. It's more difficult to win hearts. It takes time, patience, and courage, but it's worth it. What good is it having our way if it doesn't lead us to the hearts of those we love and care for? In this game of winning hearts, we have nothing to lose but our ego and fears. The sooner we set off on the road to people's hearts, particularly those who are close to us, the better. At the end of the day, what counts is whether we have been able to create our place in the hearts of people.

PEOPLE

If we keep an open mind, people we think
ordinary will surprise us with their wisdom.

RESPONSIBILITY

The burden of failure becomes lighter
when we take responsibility.

PRIORITY

When we make what is weighing on our
mind as our main priority, it saves us a lot
of energy and makes us feel lighter.

FAITH

To have unshakeable faith in the goodness and fairness of the Universal laws is a strength that no other strength can surpass.

TRUTH

The truth is not invented, it is discovered.

MIND

We cannot defeat the mind in speed. We can beat it if we remember that its one end is always in our hands.

OUR TRUE NATURE

To love and forgive is the true nature of human beings. We don't need a reason to be who we are.

However, we cannot deny that our mind is filled with all kinds of negativities that obscure our fundamental nature and we are not always loving and forgiving. How do we allow our true nature to shine through in our daily living?

Our interpersonal equations fall into three categories: people we like, and this includes people we love, admire, appreciate, people with whom we share good vibes. The second category is people we dislike, with whom we don't share good vibes. Finally, those people whom we neither like nor dislike - people we are indifferent to.

If we begin with people we actively dislike, it may be difficult to practise loving-kindness and compassion. There is too much going on here for our true nature to manifest. What we can do is to accept our responsibility and be conscious of the cost we are paying as a result of the strained relationship.

We may not know how another person is feeling, but we do know the suffering we are going through as a result of harbouring ill will in our mind.

It's better to start with the people we are indifferent to, for indifference can quickly turn into dislike if not addressed proactively. We need to relate with warmth to shift from being indifferent to being kind and considerate. We don't need a reason to be compassionate, then why wait until we find one? When we practise loving-kindness, compassion, and generosity, we are building on our true nature, which can gradually seep into our entire consciousness and shape our behaviour in day-to-day life. The key is to stop looking for a reason to be good.

Letting go of reasons to express our love and compassion in the world allows our true nature to shine through.

HUMAN

Being human is lifelong learning.

FREE WILL

Free will is like a matchstick. It should be extinguished once the fire is lit. Otherwise, it may turn into self-will.

WITNESS

When I am a "doer," life overwhelms me;
when I am a "witness," life leads me.

ENTHUSIASM

Enthusiasm is a wonderful energy
when harnessed to a purpose.

GRATITUDE

Gratitude lacks a firm foundation when we make
some people less important than others; it doesn't
waver when we treat everyone as unique.

FEAR

Ego and fear are inseparable; they follow each other
as sure as the shadow follows the substance.

FREE MIND

A free mind is a mind that is not hindered, which is not tied. In other words, when we are doing something, but something else is weighing on our mind, our mind is not free.

For example, if I am working on the computer and dinner is weighing on my mind, my mind is not free. I am lying down, but want to read a book; my mind is not free.

Gradually, working with divided attention becomes a habit, which erodes our effectiveness and enjoyment. On the other hand, when we are in sync with the activity we are engaged in, we enjoy doing it and are more efficient.

Now, let's look at the bigger picture. We cannot sustain an activity, interest or practice for a longer period if we don't enjoy it, and it's not possible to enjoy things unless we are doing them wholeheartedly with a free mind. Of course, when we start something, there are some difficulties, and expecting one would enjoy any new practice or routine right away is not realistic.

When starting a fitness practice, it is natural that one would go through physical aches and pains, and mental resistance. When starting meditation, one will find it hard to concentrate and sit for a longer period. Similarly, when starting a new job, profession or business, one would go through a learning curve that may not be all fun. However, as time goes by, we should enjoy our chosen activity or practice and look forward to it. Otherwise, it will gradually fall away.

"What if we don't enjoy the activity, but believe that it is beneficial, and there is sufficient evidence to support the belief?"

It would probably mean that we are not doing it right, perhaps there is some deficiency either in our understanding of the theory or practice, and that's normal. We all face challenges in the beginning. It's time to ask questions, clear doubts, perhaps seek guidance, read relevant material to gain a better understanding of the theory and practice. What we should not do while going through the uncertain period is to discontinue the practice. That will be like throwing the baby out with the bathwater.

As clarity begins to come and we make changes in the light of new information, knowledge, and guidance, we will not only become more adept at our practice but also enjoy it more, reaping the fruit of our hard work and sharing it with others.

FREEDOM

For human beings to experience freedom,
awareness of impermanence must become
the first response of the mind.

SPIRITUALITY

While spirituality and materialism can go
together; more of one is less of the other.

FREE

Free clouds our judgment; cost opens our eyes.

DENIAL

Denial ties us in the knots; acceptance
begins to untie the knots.

GIVE AND TAKE

If you want to give up something, take
up something you love more.

PLEASURE

It's our own pleasure that hooks us up, and then
we weave the stories to make it look nice.

DETACHMENT

The proof of the pudding is in the eating. The test of detachment is in how light we feel when we let go of our attachments.

Contemplating on "who we are not," creates the opening for detachment. Let's examine this:

We are very strongly attached to our body. We all can see our body, and if we reflect, it would seem reasonable to say "I am not my body." We get countless opportunities to remind ourselves that "I am not my body." After all, our body is always with us, although we are not always with our body. Every time we remind ourselves "I am not my body," we are creating a possibility of detachment from our body. Please remember that by saying "I am not my body," we do not deny physical existence of the body. We are simply saying we are not our body, which in a way, is obvious. It also does not mean that we will not look after or care for our body. It simply means that our clinging to our body will go away, or at least will be less, if we keep coming closer to "we are not our body" realization.

Next, our thoughts, emotions, feelings, in short, our mind. Our attachment to our point of view is as strong as our attachment to our body if not more. It doesn't seem that way because the contents of the mind are subtle than the body and not visible. Human beings are endowed with a capacity for introspection. As we develop the ability to observe our thoughts, we will be able to watch them more distinctly. When we observe our thoughts and ask ourselves the question, "Am I my thoughts?" One can honestly say, "No, I am not my thoughts." Every time we see that we are not our thoughts, we loosen our attachment to our thoughts and point of view. Here again, it would be useful to remind ourselves that we do not deny the existence of thoughts. We accept that there are thoughts, but we are not our thoughts.

Our attachment to our loved ones is no less. It is not hard to see, although difficult to accept when we are attached, that they are individuals in their own right, having their needs, priorities, and karmas.

Our possessions surround us. It may seem that things we possess are distinct from us, but we tend to identify ourselves with these possessions: kind of the car we drive, the house or apartment we live in, etc. If we go about attending to our routine, keeping in the background the question, "Who am I not?" then we will get scores of opportunities to remind ourselves that we are not our possessions. And, every time we realize it, we are driving a wedge between us and the things we possess, creating a possibility of detachment.

Is that so simple?

It's simple because that is the way things are: I am not my body. I am not my thoughts, emotions, and feelings. I am not my children or siblings or parents. I am not my possessions. It is sheer ignorance that has caused me to cling to these things, resulting in misery and suffering, which are the fruits of attachment. We just have to keep the question in our awareness. "Will we not forget?" For sure, we will. We will forget more than we will remember. It means more work, more awareness.

At the same time, it is not that simple because ignorance has put us in a deep sleep. If it were normal sleep, someone would wake us up, sometimes by splashing cold water on our face, but this is no ordinary sleep. The one who is asleep spiritually can alone wake oneself up. It is a core responsibility that a human being cannot transfer.

With "Who am I not?" in the background, we will keep dropping our body and mind continually. As we shed the baggage, we have been carrying; we will feel lighter and alive, spontaneous and free, giving and forgiving.

The more we become aware of who we are not, the more of who we are will shine through.

CHARACTER

It is not what we say but how we come across
is the real introduction of one's character.

TWINS

Harbour fear, aggression will follow; cultivate
courage, forgiveness will follow.

MIND AND MATTER

The issue is not the mind over the matter or vice versa;
the issue is who is running the show, we or our mind.

BODY

When we don't listen to our body when it's trying
to say something, it becomes a disgruntled ally.

PRESENT

Being in the present is both exhilarating and scary, the
same as someone trying to stand without crutches.

THINGS TO DO

Creating external existence, e.g., a diary, for things
we want to remember, frees up internal space
allowing us to be available in the present.

BEYOND LIKES AND DISLIKES

Likes are a milder form of greed. The expectations for likes begin on a modest scale, but they keep escalating as we start comparing. Here, we are not talking only about the social media. Our hunger for likes pervades our behaviour in all areas. We may not be able to eliminate our expectations for likes completely, but as long as we are aware of our desire to be liked and treat it with the tinge of humour, there is hope.

Similarly, dislikes are a milder form of hatred. If anything, they are more pernicious because they can lie low without being detected indefinitely. Mostly, we don't like people because they are, in some way or the other, different from us, have different opinions or views, have traits we are not able to tolerate. It's a different matter that, usually, we camouflage and reinforce our dislikes with some justification to take a high moral ground. Consider the following internal dialogue as an example:

Mind: So and so is a wrong person.

I: Why do you say that?

Mind: He lies, swears, etc.

I: True, I agree. He lies, swears, and he is rude too! Of course, he is a wrong person.

Now, I have enough reason to dislike the person. We make our decisions to dislike a person so lightly because we don't realize the cost. What we lose out on in our relationship is evident enough. We also have to put on a false front to give the impression that things are normal. But more than that, we throw away the opportunity to know the truth about ourselves, the truth that can not only save a relationship but also show us our human face, as well as the human face of others. We simply have to cross-examine ourselves a bit more closely:

Mind: So and so is a wrong person.

I: Why do you say that?

Mind: He lies, he swears, etc.

I: True, I agree...but wait a minute, haven't I too lied more than once in the past? Haven't I been angry and sworn occasionally? Don't I lose my patience from time to time and behave rudely for which I regret later?

This should be sufficient to dilute, if not dismantle, our holier than thou attitude and infuse much-needed humility in us. With humility comes the understanding regarding our faults and limitations. When we accept our weaknesses, we are better able to have tolerance for the shortcomings of others and empathize with them. Empathy leads to compassion, not dislike.

ANCHOR

We must have an anchor in our life; there is no harm if
we have more than one: meditation, prayer, teachings,
inner voice, values, and so on. Otherwise, the ship
of life is likely to flounder in the midst of storms.

ATTENTION

Attention is not thinking; attention
is what guides thinking.

LOVE

Love is not an option; it's a practical necessity, the
foundation of a happy and meaningful life.

POINT OF VIEW

To express one's point of view without disagreeing
is an art, and this art is not a play on words. It is
about genuinely appreciating other's point of view.

BLUEPRINT

What we say, or for that matter, post or forward is
a blueprint of how we should try living our life.

GOODWILL

Creating future which is filled with goodwill for
all is the best way to live a happy present.

MAKE YOUR WORLD SMALLER

We want to change everyone except ourselves. We want to make this world a better place to live in, but ignore cries of help in our backyard. We take note of others' opinions but often take for granted the views of our loved ones.

When we make our world smaller, we can deal with our lives more efficiently: real life, real people, real situations, and real problems.

More often, our conversations are centred on other people and events that have little relevance to our lives. When our interactions relate to what is happening in our lives, our relationships can become deeper and empowering. Our social gatherings too will be more purpose-oriented if we focus on how they can contribute to making our lives meaningful. We feel good coming home from a meeting or a get-together if we've learned something.

Every time we fantasize about fame, fortune, and power, we lose out on our blessings. When we make our world smaller, we begin to see the beauty of our little house, small car, little possessions, our modest talents, and beautiful people in our life.

We mostly are in the future or the past, seldom in the present. It is as if we are always in an artificial expansion mode. Making our world smaller will bring us into the present. Then we will live our daily life more mindfully, be more present to people, and will be more efficient in our work.

We strive to unravel the secrets of the Universe, go where no one has gone before, invent smarter and faster machines, replicate the natural process of creation, and yet make little effort to understand ourselves.

When we make our world the centre of our attention, we can better understand it, remain focused and feel more fulfilled.

ACCEPTANCE

At a very deep level, acceptance includes
what we cannot accept.

GENEROSITY

When you feel less than generous about
something, saying a few words of appreciation,
caring, sharing, giving, and so forth, ask yourself,
"What am I saving this for and why?"

NOW

What is unfolding now, at this moment,
is life; rest is the story of life.

Amar Ochani

TRAP

Blame and guilt are like trap doors; they open
up when we are not in the present.

WILLPOWER

The nexus between loss of control and willpower
is misplaced; loss of control always occurs
in the moment of unconsciousness.

KARMAS

No one can, and no one may interfere in the karmas
of others; when we are kind and compassionate,
we are working on our own karmas.

NATURE OF EXISTENCE

Do we experience peace and joy when we live life unconsciously, immersed in material comforts, and tied to attachments?

The material things can give us satisfaction temporarily. When we feel hungry, we need to eat. That will keep us satisfied for some time until we feel hungry again. The same goes with other necessities and comforts of life. They have an important role to play in our lives. However, they cannot help us get over the feeling of unsatisfactoriness in life. Whether we live in a hut or a palace, drive a big or a small car, have zero balance at the end of the week or millions, we cannot get over the feeling of unease that keeps surfacing in our life again and again. And, it's good that such a feeling surfaces for then, we can do something about it.

We live under the illusion that if we fix what is not working, our life will be complete and we will get over the feeling of emptiness. We fix something and then realize that something else needs fixing. The process goes on until finally, the time comes when we get set for good.

The problem is not with the issues. Issues are a matter of manageability. The real question is the nature of existence itself. It's the glass which is bound to break one day, but we are unwilling to engage in this issue. Death will not go away by merely ignoring it any more than fear by suppressing it. We need to address this issue, not for the sake of death but because accepting its inevitability and integrating it into our day-to-day life can transform our life experience.

If we see the glass as already broken, it will loosen our attachment to the glass. We will continue to use and enjoy it, take its due care but we will be free from the fear that it'll break some day. And finally when it breaks down, we may feel a little bit sad, but we will not be heartbroken for we knew all along that it was made to break.

Existence comes to an end not because something went wrong, but because "ending" is ingrained in existence. It is just that we forget it and live as if we will be here forever. The result is our deep attachment, clinging to life, which is the main cause of our suffering. Freedom comes when we awaken to the reality of life in our everyday living and strive to liberate ourselves from the illusion of permanence.

As Eckhart Tolle has said: «The secret of life is to die before you die - and find that there is no death." Simple yet life-changing words.

HUMILITY

Knowledge, insight or wisdom should be accompanied
by humility lest the arrogance shuts the door.

PEACE

Peace comes when we accept the way we are; we
lose it when we try to justify the way we are.

WALKING ALONE

The first condition of walking on the right
path is the readiness to walk alone.

RHETORIC

Rhetoric betrays our insincerity that
is obvious to all except us.

HINDSIGHT

From hindsight, we could have done everything
better; this is the mind's way of making us feel bad.

MIND

The mind can't see the difference between real and
unreal; that is why it always tries to re-write the
past and create the future in its own image.

COMMITMENT

Miracles happen in the space of commitment: Limitations vanish, and new possibilities emerge. Imbued with a sense of commitment, we stop giving reasons and instead, show results.

Time management and punctuality are the byproducts of commitment. As hard as we may try, it's not possible to manage time efficiently or be consistently punctual if we are not committed to the cause we espouse or a task we undertake.

Relationships wither away due to a lack of commitment. Likes and dislikes are changeable. The spirit of commitment alone can survive the rough winds of reality.

Commitment helps us to be on purpose. It takes away struggle from our daily living. We will be more focused on our short-term and long-term goals. We will waste less time and be more productive. Nothing is too small when done in the context of commitment.

As we integrate commitment in our daily living, we will see that we can deliver on promises, are more effective at our workplaces, and people trust us more. Our self-esteem is enhanced, and we feel fulfilled. It gives back power to us, where it belongs.

STRENGTHS AND WEAKNESSES

We see in others the strengths we wish for;
the weaknesses we wish we hadn't.

HUMAN BEINGS

Human beings were designed for less: less talk, less eating,
less doing, and more being. We have turned it upside
down with the result we are more machine than human.

PEOPLE

Don't be impressed by the good people
and have an aversion to bad people; good
and bad are changing phenomena.

DREAMS

There are better chances of our dreams coming
true when we include others in our dreams.

COMPASSION

Those who seem to deserve less, need more compassion.

PURIFICATION

Inner purification requires hard work and
patience, the same as a cloth that has
gathered a lot of dust over a long time.

LIVE LIGHTLY

When the whisper is good enough, why raise one's voice. When the quiet voice in the heart says, it's all well, why look anywhere else to find peace. When the present moment is all we have, why carry the burden of past and anxieties about future?

We habitually use more force than what is required doing our routine activities such as eating, sitting, walking, shutting the doors, washing dishes, holding things, etc. We don't have to handle everything in an overly forceful way. We can enjoy our daily activities more if we perform them with light touch losing none of the effectiveness.

Analyzing and comparing have their role in our life, for example, when we are solving a problem or planning something. However, we don't need them all the time. Instead, we can use the power of observation. Observation is the soft face of mind and is sufficient for most of the routine activities. Observation consumes the fraction of the energy we need for analysis and comparison. We feel relaxed and at peace when we observe without judging and comparing.

Harsh words are heavy and leave the trail of bitterness behind. On speaking gently, the Buddha said, "Speak quietly to everyone, and they too will be gentle in their speech. Harsh words hurt and come back to the speaker."

The way we relate to our thoughts is equally important. We differentiate between negative and positive thoughts treating negative thoughts as the bad apples to be weeded out. It seems quite reasonable also. While there can be no doubt that our goal in life should be to cultivate wholesome and positive thoughts and rid ourselves of unwholesome and negative thoughts, when we try to suppress negative thoughts or try to eliminate them by force, they come back to torment us with double vigour. There is oft-repeated saying "resistance causes persistence." When we observe negative thoughts lightly with bare attention, they will lose their energy and gradually become weaker and weaker.

When we live lightly, we are in the dance with life in slow motion enjoying every move. It is like caressing the object of our attention. We can eliminate much of stress and struggle by cultivating the power of observation.

LIFE

Life doesn't become messy in a day; it takes the time **to reap the harvest of wrong actions.**

IMPERMANENCE

To search for the missing link to arrive at peace is futile. Nothing is permanent; experience this, and you have arrived.

HAPPINESS

Happiness is a habit; same as unhappiness, except, it is hard to break the habit of unhappiness.

THE UNIVERSE

We feel alone when we forget that the Universe is
always waiting to extend its helping hand to us.

PASSION

Once you discover what makes you happy and
fulfilled, guard it as a mother guards her child.

WISDOM

Wisdom is not in succeeding; wisdom is in
moving on when we don't succeed.

KEEPING UP THE APPEARANCES

The biggest stress in life is trying to keep up the appearances. We erect the facade of perfection and niceness around us and then live rest of our lives hiding behind it. Being nice to people is great! It is the humane way to relate to fellow beings. However, when we are nice because we want to look good, we become selective. Then we worship the high and mighty and ignore the humble; kowtow the influential and shrug off the lesser known. It may give us worldly success and make us socially mobile, but it leaves us empty inside.

When we try to live our life as we are rather than to fit in, we are authentic. Then we don't have to wear a mask to look good or keep up the appearances. We still have to work and pay our bills, but that doesn't come in the way of living an authentic life.

The key ingredient of living an authentic life is courage. The courage to own one's humanity in all its shades: good and bad, beautiful and ugly, courage to be vulnerable. The vulnerability is the essence of being human; it's allowing people in our lives to get a peep into who we are.

We can be authentic and yet act appropriately. We will be relevant to situations, people, and places, but we will not try to be someone we are not or say something we don't believe. It means we choose to live our life with honesty and have the courage to practise it in our day to day life.

There is more to authentic living. Often, we shy away from taking the stand and are hesitant to say or do what we think is right. Living life courageously and authentically creates a possibility of taking the stand on what we believe is right in a responsible manner. It is easier to express one's point of view honestly if one doesn't have to hide a skeleton in the cupboard.

Authentic living takes away the compulsion to prove oneself and leads to peace, joy, and aliveness in life. It's a better choice.

LITTLE BY LITTLE

There is a lot to do and a long way to go,
but a task becomes lighter and distances
shorter when we do it little by little.

TRUTH

Truth without courage is like a seed without soil.

WORDS

The picture painted by words is always incomplete; it
becomes complete when we see what is unsaid in words.

SELF-CONFIDENCE

The measure of self-confidence is deeds, not words.

SILENCE

Sweetest sound is the sound of silence.

GOODNESS

While being right and being good may not be opposed to each other, the compulsion to be right often comes in the way of being good.

ATTITUDE

When we see deficiencies of the people, we limit ourselves; when we see their strengths, it makes us bigger. Impatience and intolerance are the fruits of former; compassion and tolerance are the blessings of latter.

Once we make the negative conclusion about a person, our mind looks for and tries to find the evidence to support the conclusion we have reached. Eventually, a point is reached when we stop listening or seeing anything positive about that person and consequently, lose a valuable resource in our life. Moreover, it doesn't make anyone happy.

However, It's a fact of life that there are people we disagree or don't vibe well with. It's not uncommon to hear the remark "I just can't stand that person! And I can't help it." What do we do then?

The first thing to realize is that with this attitude, we are the net losers. Inevitably, the consequences will surface and the day of reckoning will arrive. This should bring in focus the cost of our attitude.

The next is to accept that it's our problem, not theirs. It may be because we don't know a person well enough or there is a lack of communication. Or, maybe we are not able to arouse empathy and loving kindness for the individual, or there is some karmic load or debt. We may not know for sure, but we will not help the situation if we turn it into blame and guilt game.

We can very well distance ourselves from the people when we feel it's not working until we have given time, time to heal. But sometimes it's not possible, mainly, in work situations or when we share a responsibility to get things done. In such circumstances, the best option is to seek out the help until we have sorted out our attitude or learned our lessons the hard way.

HUMAN BIRTH

When I think what I have, there's never
enough; when I begin to think who I am,
then I have an incredible opportunity!

ABUNDANCE

Insufficiency, not abundance is the normal human
experience. To experience abundance, keep giving all
you can, and that all doesn't have to be money alone.

FOCUS

If we focus on others, we will continue tying the knots;
if we focus on ourselves, we will untie the knots.

ATTACHMENT

We get attached to what is not ours
in the first place and suffer.

PREJUDICES

We become prisoners of our prejudices;
no one can set us free if we don't.

FORGIVENESS

Forgiveness begins with self and
then flows towards others.

BELIEF SYSTEM

Two worlds - one that we know and are conscious of. And another that is unknown to us, that which we call unconscious, or subconscious. It is said that 95% percent of our mind-brain activity is beyond our conscious awareness. This wouldn't concern us, and we can safely ignore what is buried in our unconscious if it were not affecting us in our life. On the contrary, our lives are run by the beliefs and values that we were taught, or we picked up, mostly unconsciously, in our childhood. We may not be aware, but the belief systems we unknowingly internalized run the show and will continue to run the show for the rest of our life unless we do something about it.

There is always something cooking in the unconscious, but we come to know when it reaches the boiling point, and by then it's too late. We make New Year resolutions, read books on positive thinking, listen to motivational speakers, but lessons learned are forgotten too soon. The affirmations we make are short-lived. Bombardment of self-help videos on social media doesn't even scratch the surface. We set up goals that look good only on paper. It is as if there is an undercurrent or stream of thoughts that is continuously running under our every conscious activity and is not in sync with it. The force of the undercurrent is so strong that we willy-nilly get carried away by it. Five percent is always at the mercy of ninety-five percent.

Now imagine what would become possible if we harness the power of the unconscious? What sort of power can we put in our every conscious action if the power of unconscious gets aligned with it? Then the conscious and unconscious don't work at cross-purposes. Then we don't have to swim against the current. Instead, we use the force that was working against us, in our favour.

Once we get a glimpse of how we unconsciously sabotage our efforts, we begin to get a handle on our unconscious mind.

The first step is to observe how the two worlds are pitted against each other. We want to make millions and a voice in our head says, "Not possible; you are a very unlucky person." Or, one wants to become a public speaker, and a voice in their unconscious says, "No one likes you, how can you become a public speaker?" Or, we want to speak out our mind, and a voice in our head says, "Play safe, be practical."

Next, we have to go deeper to uncover the underlying beliefs. For instance, I have an altercation with a friend. I have an excellent explanation to calm him, but I don't try to explain. Instead, I say, "What is the point, he will never understand." If I stop here, hard feelings will only turn harder and sour the relationship as time passes by. However, if I look deeper, I may discover that underneath that attitude is my self-limiting belief that people don't understand me, and they will never understand me. Now, this is an insight that can change me forever if I earnestly work on it. Then I can re-write my self-belief - that if I try sincerely, people will understand me or whatever fits my vision.

Having observed how self-defeating beliefs sabotage our efforts and plans, the next step is to see that it is us who put together our belief system, albeit unconsciously. So long as we are not aware, they will continue to run our lives leaving a trail of frustrations and disappointments.

Now, we have laid the foundation and are ready to replace the beliefs that come in the way of realizing our dreams with those that help us in achieving our goals and living a life that fulfills us. If we are committed to creating breakthroughs and live a life that we always wanted to live, we must develop the beliefs that support us in our mission.

LEARNING

Learning is of two kinds; learning to get
better and learning to become wise. Former
breeds arrogance; latter, humility.

EQUANIMITY

It's not about being happy or sad; it's about being at peace
when we are happy, and being at peace when we are sad.

UNIQUE

There is no doubt you are unique,
but then so is everyone else.

LOVING KINDNESS

Loving-kindness is a shortcut to peace.

BLESSINGS

Things we receive without asking are the things that matter most - air, the sun, water, and of course, love!

LISTENING

If you want people to listen to you,
listen to them; it's that simple.

SUFFERING IS OPTIONAL

Suffering is optional because it is self-created. It's, therefore, reasonable to say that we alone can end it.

Everything has a cause except that we don't pause to find one. Suffering starts when we harbour negative thoughts. It gets deeper and deeper as we try looking for the culprit in the wrong places - externally. The clarity dawns when we sit back and reflect upon the situation with an open mind.

Optimism and its corollary sense of well-being are, to a great extent, the result of faith in the essential goodness of people. When doubt replaces faith, it brings suffering in its wake. It's necessary to resolve our doubts as they arise lest they get entrenched and cloud our judgment.

It is said human beings are, by nature, social animals. We cannot avoid associating with people. With association come expectations, and as we know, expectations are the primary cause of suffering. While we should have goodwill and compassion for everyone, we only have so much time and energy, and we should use these wisely to advance the purpose of our life.

The same goes for action. As long as we live, we must perform our action. An action carried out with a selfish desire for its fruit is a breeding ground for suffering. We must, therefore, act selflessly and do our duty without selfish attachment to the "fruit" of an action - as Lord Krishna advises Prince Arjuna in Bhagwad Gita.

There will still be problems and breakdowns in our life from time to time. That's life. However, we can minimize the impact of the problems and the pain of suffering in the event of breakdowns if we own up to our responsibility and communicate with honesty and sincerity.

RESPONSE

There are two kinds of responses: emotional
and thoughtful; the former is rooted in
attachment, latter, in wisdom.

SELF-DISCOVERY

Every mistake, followed by a correction is
an opportunity for self-discovery.

VISION

The vision when shared ceases to be personal; then
it is owned by everyone who is touched by it.

SECRET

It's a secret that we all know, but don't want to
know: If I am suffering, it's because I have done
something wrong; if I am happy, it's because I
have done something right. Rest is all noise.

NOBLE BEING

When we genuinely feel happy in the happiness of others,
we have come a long way to abide in our true nature.

CHANGE

Change at the root level is always gradual. It's
like a mango tree that bears fruit over a period of
years. However, if we have planted a sweet seed
or seedling, it will only give sweet mangoes.

THIRD DIMENSION

The first dimension of the existence is our body, home of sensations and feelings. The second dimension is the mind and its contents: thoughts, the world of I, me, and mine, a.k.a the ego, moods, emotions, judgments, etc. These worlds are always in flux, constantly changing.

When we see ourselves distinct from our body and mind, we have created the third dimension of the existence to dwell in and operate from in the world. This is the home of free will, the springboard of unconditioned action. Herein lies the power of determination, the possibility of being other than who we have always been. This is the space of awareness.

Any attempt at the definition of this space dilutes its power. We try to define what is beyond words without experiencing the true nature of first and second dimension and get ourselves entangled in the web of intellectual polemics and endless arguments. Access to the third dimension: space of awareness does not happen by ignoring the mind and body, but by traversing the entire field of mind and body, by experiencing their fragile and transitory nature.

Dwelling in the space of awareness, as much as possible, allows us to live powerfully in the world, as well as remain equanimous in the face of ups and downs. As regards the question whether this space is atman, self, self with the lowercase or uppercase 's'; whether it is mortal or immortal, etc., these issues are better left alone as they, instead of helping, come in the way of our using this space to break free from the bondage of conditioned mind and deep attachment to the body.

Regular practice of meditation, being mindful in day-to-day life, and contemplation of the true nature of things can help us glimpse the third dimension and experience the internal peace and joy that no material object can match.

ACKNOWLEDGMENTS

This book would not have been possible without kind words and valuable feedback from the readers of my "Thought for the Day" and "Thought for the Week" over three years. This work indeed is the result of shared vision – I thank each one of you with all my heart.

Special thanks to Marisha Karwa for painstakingly editing the book and providing the thoughtful input when most needed. Thanks are also due to Krishna Bectorji for his valuable suggestions. I also want to thank all those who have contributed in one way or another to the publishing of this book but whose names are not mentioned.

My family provided steady support throughout this exciting adventure. Their love and smiles kept me energized. My wife, Komal helped me through the entire process by providing moral support, and valuable suggestions that often revealed the angles I had overlooked in my enthusiasm. Her contribution in making this book happen is no less than mine.

ABOUT THE AUTHOR

Amar Ochani grew up in Mumbai, India. He did his post-graduation in political science from Bombay University and lived and worked in London, UK before settling down in Canada. He has led various seminars for the Landmark Forum in India. His "Thought for the day" and "Thought for the Week" have been well received by readers. This is his first collection of essays and thoughts. He lives in Coquitlam, BC, Canada, with his wife.

Made in the USA
Columbia, SC
21 July 2018